# VITAL SIGNS 1992

## The Trends That Are Shaping Our Future

Lester R. Brown
Christopher Flavin
Hal Kane

Editor: Linda Starke

with Ed Ayres
Alan Thein Durning
Jodi L. Jacobson
Nicholas Lenssen
Marcia Lowe
Michael Renner
Howard Youth

W. W. Norton & Company
New York London

Copyright © 1992 by Worldwatch Institute

The text of this book is composed in Garth Graphic with the
display set in Industria Alternate.
Composition and manufacturing by the Haddon Craftsmen, Inc.
Book design by Charlotte Staub.

ISBN 0-393-03453-4 (cl)
ISBN 0-393-30974-6 (pa)

W. W. Norton & Company, Inc.,
500 Fifth Avenue, New York, N.Y. 10110
W. W. Norton & Company Ltd.,
10 Coptic Street, London WC1A 1PU

1 2 3 4 5 6 7 8 9 0

 This book is printed on recycled paper

# VITAL
# SIGNS
## 1992

# CONTENTS

ACKNOWLEDGMENTS   9
FOREWORD   11
OVERVIEW:
ENTERING A NEW ERA   15
   Promising New Trends   16
   Food Trend Reversals   17
   Diverging Energy Trends   18
   Social Trends   19

## Part One: KEY INDICATORS

FOOD TRENDS   23
   Grain Harvest Drops   24
   Soybean Production Up   26
   Meat Production Rises   28
   Fish Catch Falls   30
   Grain Stocks Decline   32

AGRICULTURAL RESOURCE
TRENDS   35
   Grainland Shrinks   36
   Irrigation Expansion Slowing   38
   Fertilizer Use Falls   40

ENERGY TRENDS   43
   Oil Production Falls   44
   Natural Gas Production Climbs   46
   Nuclear Power at Standstill   48
   Wind Power Soars   50
   Solar Cell Production Expanding   52
   Energy Efficiency Falls   54

ATMOSPHERIC TRENDS   57
   Global Temperature Rises   58
   Carbon Emissions Steady   60
   CFC Production Falling Fast   62

ECONOMIC TRENDS   65
   Economy Contracts Slightly   66
   Third World Debt Persists   68
   Automobile Production Drops   70
   Bicycle Production Outpaces Autos   72

SOCIAL TRENDS   75
   Population Growth Sets Record   76
   Infant Mortality Declining   78
   Cigarette Smoking Losing Favor   80

MILITARY TRENDS   83
   Military Expenditures Falling   84
   Nuclear Arsenal Shrinking   86

# Part Two: SPECIAL FEATURES

ENVIRONMENTAL
FEATURES 91
Birds Fast Disappearing 92
Forests Shrinking at Record Rate 94
U.S. Soil Erosion Cut 96
Steel Recycling Rising Slowly 98
Nuclear Waste Accumulating 100

ECONOMIC FEATURES 103
Arms Trade Exceeds Grain 104
Wheat/Oil Exchange Rate Shifts 106

SOCIAL FEATURES 109
Income Distribution Worsening 110
Maternal Mortality Takes Heavy
Toll 112
Coerced Motherhood Increasing 114

NOTES 117

# ACKNOWLEDGMENTS

Producing a volume covering as many issues as this one does depends on a lot of help from many sources. The authors wish to thank those who assisted with the extensive research required, including Vikram Akula, Derek Denniston, Vicki Elkin, Megan Ryan, and Marnie Stetson.

Several individuals outside the Institute read the entire manuscript and offered suggestions for improving it. These included Herman Daly, Robert Goodland, Dana Meadows, Gail Finsterbusch, and Maureen Hinkle. Not only did these reviewers provide useful comments, but they did it quickly, providing support for the adage that the best way to get something done is to give it to a busy person. Among those who brought their expertise to bear on specific sections are Paul Gipe, Gerd Hagmeyer-Gaverus, Carl Haub, Franklyn Holzman, Tom Kearney, Paul Maycock, Mack McFarland, Stan Norris, Eric Phillips, and Somnath Sen. We are grateful to all for helping improve the quality of the manuscript.

We are indebted to Reah Janise Kauffman for coordinating manuscript production, a task that is complicated by the profusion of tables and figures throughout the book.

Linda Starke, who has edited each of our nine annual *State of the World* reports, also edited this volume. Her experience was invaluable, a resource on which we relied heavily. And when she was busy at the '92 Global Forum in Rio, Ed Ayres, editor of the Worldwatch Papers, stepped in at the production stage to keep the process moving smoothly.

We would like to thank the Surdna Foundation for launching this annual series with a $150,000 startup grant. We are particularly indebted to Surdna executive director Edward Skloot, who was one of the first to see its potential for helping to shape the policies needed to build a sustainable future. For his personal encouragement and enthusiastic support, we are deeply grateful. In addition to the startup grant from the Surdna Foundation, the W. Alton Jones Foundation is also providing direct project support.

While Surdna and W. Alton Jones provided project funding for *Vital Signs,* the volume draws heavily on the Institute's extensive information-gathering network and its on-going research. These resources are made possible by several general support grants. Among the supporting foundations are Geraldine R. Dodge, William and Flora Hewlett, Andrew W. Mellon, Edward John Noble, and Frank Weeden. Additional sources of general support include the Lynn and Karl Prickett Fund, Rockefeller Brothers Fund, and Winthrop Rockefeller Trust. Personal grants for general support came from Turki al Faisal and Roy Young. This project was also abetted by information gathered and research done as part of projects supported by the George Gund, John D. and Catherine T. MacArthur, Curtis and Edith Munson, and Public Welfare foundations, and the U.N. Population Fund.

Lester R. Brown
Christopher Flavin
Hal Kane

9

# FOREWORD

As the environmental era has unfolded in recent decades, the need for a new set of indicators has emerged. But the official response lags far behind in both national governments and the U.N. complex of agencies. As the global economy has become unsustainable, damaging and destroying the natural systems and resources that support it, there is a need to identify and measure destructive trends such as chlorofluorocarbon (CFC) production, acid rain, carbon dioxide emissions, and deforestation. Equally important is the need to measure the efforts to reverse them, such as production of CFC substitutes and investments in the development of renewable energy resources.

What societies carefully measure today are often trends that belong to an earlier era. They bear little relationship to the interaction of the environmental, demographic, and economic forces now shaping our lives and those of our children. They may be of only marginal value to the most important decisions being made by individuals, governments, and businesses in the late twentieth and early twenty-first centuries.

Every day, for example, the business sections of leading U.S. newspapers devote two square inches of space to changes in the price of pork bellies the day before, but only occasionally do they refer to the massive loss of plant and animal species that is undermining the global economy. Similarly, new housing starts are reported each month, but no one regularly reports on the clearcutting of forests that provided the wood—or on the soil erosion, silting of rivers, and destruction of fisheries associated with the cutting.

In the United States, the Motor Vehicle Manufacturers Association releases data on automobile sales every 10 days, information religiously reported in the daily newspapers, but there is no similar report on bicycle sales, even on an annual basis. Yet at the global level, bicycles serve far more people and their use is growing more rapidly than that of cars.

For many trends, no one is officially responsible for compiling annual data and making them publicly available. For example, carbon emissions from burning fossil fuels and forests will quite literally reshape the earth's climatic system, altering daily weather patterns, yet there is no United Nations annual report on carbon emissions. Similarly, many of us are concerned about what is happening to the ozone layer that protects life on earth from harmful ultraviolet radiation. Is CFC production still rising or has it begun to decline, as international agreements would imply? Is anyone monitoring the effect of wind and water erosion on the thin layer of topsoil that supplies most of our food?

Sometimes official agencies assiduously gather data, but then publish it in a statistical yearbook, with little analysis of trends. One such example is the information gathered by the U.N. Food and Agriculture Organization in Rome on the oceanic fish catch. These data are reported in great detail, by country and species, but little energy is devoted to fostering public understanding of the trends. The data are important not merely because they measure fish supplies, but because changes in the catch can provide insights into the biological carrying capacity of one of the world's major ecosystems.

With some indicators, private groups have stepped in to fill the gap. The most reliable source of data on global military expenditures, for example, is the Stockholm International Peace Research Institute. Without the information compiled by this group, the world would have to rely on data made available by national governments, much of it biased for security reasons. Getting behind the security blanket to obtain real numbers for some countries takes an enormous effort.

*Vital Signs* is designed to fill some of these gaps in the official gathering, analysis, and dissemination of global environmental data. At present, coverage of economic trends dwarfs that of environmental ones, though the latter are arguably more important. This is largely because governments and industries regularly collect and release data on dozens of economic indicators, such as employment, industrial output, and interest rates, while details of global environmental trends, such as deforestation, are collected only once a decade. Our goal is to supply information that will, in a small way, redress the enormous imbalance in coverage of economic and environmental trends and issues.

The book is divided into two major sections. Part One contains trends for which historical global data are available, such as oil production, the oceanic fish catch, or population growth. Each is presented in two pages, one of text and one with data and graphs.

Part Two contains essays on trends that are obviously important but for which historical global data are not available. For example, there are no annual data on the loss of plant and animal species. Thus this topic falls in the special features section, where this year we include a brief discussion on what is known of bird population declines and species losses. Occasionally there are also trends we wish to compare, such as grain exports and arms exports. Part Two permits a more detailed discussion of such comparisons than is possible in Part One.

From year to year the content of *Vital Signs* will vary somewhat. A core group of indicators, including such trends as grain production, carbon emissions, and population growth, will appear each time. Other measures will vary from one edition to the next. Over time we will likely expand the number of indicators as we gain a better sense of the official gaps in the global information gathering and dissemination system.

We see *Vital Signs* as a companion to our annual *State of the World* report, a way of providing up-to-date annual information on far more topics than would otherwise be possible. Our hope is that it will eventually be translated into all of the 26 languages in which *State of the World* now appears.

We hope that this volume will meet many needs: that national governments will use it to compare their efforts to reduce carbon emissions or soil erosion with those for the world as a whole; that industrial firms will use it to compare the share of recycled materials in their output with that of the rest of the world; and that individuals who are helping establish bicycle-friendly transportation systems will be interested in the global trends in the use of bicycles and automobiles. More generally, we hope that not only environmental activists but concerned citizens everywhere will want to find out whether population growth is slowing, how rapidly CFC production is being phased out, or whether the world's nuclear arsenal is shrinking, as disarmament agreements promised.

Our aim is to produce an accessible annual volume that will both be read widely and also be used as a reference, kept close at hand for when a key number or trend is needed. We hope that reporters and editors in both the print and electronic media will find this an invaluable aid, something to be referred to frequently. For editors, we hope that *Vital Signs* will also be a source of story ideas. And finally, we hope it will be a volume whose publication is eagerly awaited each year as more and more people personally track the trends that are shaping the world in which we and our children will live.

Your suggestions and comments are welcome.

Lester R. Brown     Worldwatch Institute
June 1992     1776 Massachusetts Ave., N.W.
     Washington DC 20036

# VITAL
# SIGNS
## 1992

# OVERVIEW
## Entering a New Era

## Lester R. Brown

Anyone who reads newspapers, listens to the radio, or watches television knows—or at least senses—that civilization is in trouble. This feeling comes not only from news about what is happening to the earth's protective ozone layer, for example, but also from daily experiences—the polluted air that is impairing our children's respiratory systems, or the price we pay for seafood, or the distance we must now walk to find firewood to cook the evening meal.

Clearly, these experiences are a result of the unprecedented expansion of human numbers and economic activity that has occurred since mid-century. Since then our numbers have more than doubled—from 2.5 to 5.5 billion. The global output of goods and services has expanded nearly fivefold. This growth in economic activity, and the technologies used to achieve it, are damaging the planet, raising doubts about its capacity to sustain future improvements in the human condition.

The destruction under way takes many forms. We see it in the sick and dying forests of Central Europe, the burning off of Brazilian rain forests by cattle ranchers, the destruction of forests in India and in semiarid Africa by firewood gatherers, and the clear-cutting of tropical hardwoods in Southeast Asia by loggers.

We see it in the acidification of lakes in the northern tier of industrial countries. We see it in the death of the Aral Sea, which once yielded 100 million pounds of fish a year. Even the vast Mediterranean is deteriorating from the human onslaught, and may finally succumb. We see the deterioration of the planet in the desertification of Africa and India. We see it in the uninhabitability of thousands of toxic waste sites and "temporary" nuclear waste storage facilities. We feel the change in the hotter summers of the last decade. We measure it in the increasing amount of ultraviolet radiation reaching the earth's surface.

We have inadvertently acquired a great deal of influence over the future habitability of the planet. At issue is whether we can assume the responsibility to go with it. In many respects, this is the question for our generation. If we cannot reverse the trends that are undermining our future, environmental deterioration and economic decline may soon start to feed on each other, depriving future generations of the opportunity to support themselves.

Assuming responsibility for the mess we have made begins with measurement of physical changes in the planet's life-support systems that we have set in motion. Such understanding is necessary, though by no means sufficient, for wise policymaking. At the same time, we need to measure and chart our progress, or lack thereof, in reversing the degradation.

We know that global environmental trends over the last few decades have not been favorable. We have witnessed, and indeed caused, an acceleration of several trends, including deforestation, the loss of plant and animal species, soil erosion, stratospheric ozone depletion, and the buildup of greenhouse gases in the atmosphere. There are, however, some positive trends beginning to emerge. We need to be aware of these

15

and to build on them, eventually achieving a momentum that will reverse the degradation and set the world on a sustainable path.

## PROMISING NEW TRENDS

Among the most promising developments in recent years are the wholesale dismantling of nuclear weapons, the decline in global military expenditures, the dramatic reduction in chlorofluorocarbon (CFC) production, the growth in bicycle production, and the decline in cigarette smoking. Some of these are lead indicators, measurements of change that can set in motion other changes. The decline in military expenditures, for example, may free up resources for investment in family planning or reforestation. Similarly, the drop in CFC production presages a decline in emissions. This in turn will slow depletion of the ozone layer over a period of several decades and, if CFC use is phased out entirely, lead to eventual healing of the ozone layer. But it will take many decades before the rising amount of ultraviolet radiation reaching the earth is reversed.

In many ways, the recent shrinkage in the world's nuclear arsenal is the most promising trend since the first nuclear bombs were dropped nearly a half-century ago. In 1991 the number of strategic nuclear warheads was reduced from some 23,700 to 19,200—a decline of 19 percent. (See pages 86–87.) The end of the cold war, budgetary constraints, and the discovery of widespread radioactive pollution around nuclear weapons manufacturing facilities in both the United States and the former Soviet Union have all contributed to the reduction. Although dismantling nuclear weapons and dealing with the radioactive materials they contain is not easy, it is clearly an exciting trend, one that raises hope of an eventual end to the threat of nuclear warfare.

Closely related to the planned shrinkage of the nuclear arsenal is the decline in global military expenditures. (See pages 84–85.) After increasing every year from 1960 until 1989, these expenditures dropped an estimated 6 percent in 1990. When 1991 tabulations are complete, they are likely to show another drop of comparable magnitude. Although 6 percent may not seem like much, it amounts to some $56 billion, a sum that exceeds expenditures on reforestation, soil conservation, and family planning in the Third World. If efforts to strengthen the U.N. peacekeeping capacity continue, this could be just the beginning of an ongoing decline in global military expenditures.

Perhaps the most impressive achievement in terms of the extensive international cooperation needed has been the reduced output of CFCs, the family of chemicals that is depleting the stratospheric ozone layer. (See pages 62–63.) Three years after British scientists stationed in Antarctica first reported the hole in the ozone layer in 1985, the production of CFCs peaked. Since the 1988 record, production has fallen some 46 percent. It is a dramatic success, a potential model for dealing with other global issues.

Human mobility has risen dramatically during the last 15 years, largely because of the vast growth in the world bicycle fleet. (See pages 72–73.) Between 1960 and 1990, annual world bicycle production increased from 20 million to an estimated 95 million. In western industrial societies, transportation systems are auto-centered, but for the world as a whole, the bicycle is the leading vehicle for personal transportation. In China, whose population nearly matches that of the entire industrial world, the bicycle completely dominates transportation systems, outnumbering automobiles by some 200 to 1. This, combined with the extensive reliance on bikes in other populous countries, such as Japan and India, has propelled this form of transportation into the lead. The bicycle's growing popularity lies in its responsiveness to many contemporary problems, including air pollution, acid rain, traffic congestion, and the need for exercise, particularly among those in societies where lifestyles are highly sedentary.

Among the most promising new social trends is the world decline in cigarettes smoked per adult of 1.5 percent between 1988 and 1991. (See pages 80–81.) Leading this decline are western industrial countries, importantly the United States and Canada, where consumption per adult is now dropping several percent each year. U.S. government-funded health research, linking 40 percent of all cancers to smoking and establishing cigarettes as a major cause of heart disease and strokes, is driving the campaign against smoking. Bans on advertising, prohibitions on smoking in public places, and rising cigarette taxes are all contributing to this promising trend.

FOOD TREND REVERSALS

The era of dramatic rises in per capita production of basic foodstuffs such as grain, soybeans, meat, and fish—which roughly spanned 1950 to 1985—has apparently come to an end, replaced by a new era in which production per person is either static or declining. The new trends emerging are not reassuring, particularly for the billion or so people on the lower rungs of the global economic ladder.

By far the most important indicator is grain production per person. (See pages 24–25.) After rising nearly 3 percent per year from 1950 to the peak year of 1984, it has expanded since then at scarcely 1 percent a year. As a result, output per person is slowly declining.

More immediately, the drop in grain production in 1991 of 84 million tons was the largest year-to-year drop in history. The effect of this drop on consumption in 1992 is being cushioned somewhat by a projected drawdown on world grain stocks of some 27 million tons. (See pages 32–33.) Nonetheless, even after adjusting for this, U.S. Department of Agriculture data show that the world is facing a record fall in grain consumption per person of nearly 3 percent in 1992, a drop that may depress grain consumption among some of the world's poor below the survival level. In terms of sheer numbers, the greatest suffering is expected in the 43 countries, home to more than 800 million people, where incomes have been falling for at least a decade. For them, making it to the next harvest has become an ongoing struggle. And in Southern Africa, drought has caused an immediate food crisis.

Contributing to the slower growth in grain output is both the dearth of new land suitable for producing grain and much slower growth in irrigated area and fertilizer use over the last decade. (See pages 38–41.) The latter is due, in large part, to the declining response of grain yields to additional fertilizer use in agriculturally advanced countries. In the former Soviet Republics, economic reforms that boosted fertilizer prices to world market levels have sharply lowered fertilizer use.

Growth in soybean production, the world's leading protein crop, has slowed dramatically over the last dozen years. (See pages 26–27.) Since soybeans are a legume with a built-in nitrogen supply, their yields are not as responsive to the use of chemical fertilizers as those of grain are. As a result, farmers get more soybeans largely by planting more. But finding the land for this is becoming increasingly difficult, often coming at the expense of other crops.

With meat production, growth in output has also slowed in recent years. (See pages 28–29.) After rising by nearly four fifths between 1950 and 1987, meat production per person has levelled off, neither increasing nor decreasing over the last five years. The shift in the composition of world meat production during the last 41 years is environmentally revealing. In 1950, the production of beef and mutton, nearly all of it from grass and other forage, accounted for more than half the world meat supply. Over time, however, as the herds and flocks began to push against the grazing limits of rangelands, the growth in meat production came more and more from grain. As farmers realized it took some seven pounds of grain to produce a pound of beef in a feedlot, but only four pounds to produce a pound of pork and scarcely two for a pound of chicken, production gains shifted to the more efficient converters.

Between 1950 and 1991, mutton production, including both sheep and goats, barely doubled, that of beef increased 2.7 times, that of pork 4.5 times, and that of poultry more than 9 times. During the period when grain and soybean production were increasing rapidly, it was relatively easy to expand meat production, but now that per capita production of grain is slowly declining and that of soybeans has levelled off, this will be much more difficult.

While the growth in meat production has been slowing, so too has that of the fish catch. (See pages 30–31.) In 1989, the world fish catch reached a record 100 million tons, the maximum that marine biologists believe that oceanic fisheries can sustain. If they are right, a decline in per capita seafood consumption is virtually inevitable, even assuming a steady expansion of fish farming. This will likely put even more upward pressure on the price of seafood, which, after adjusting for inflation, has doubled over the last few decades while beef and poultry prices have remained more or less constant.

These new trends raise profound questions: How will governments respond to falling per capita production of commodities so essential to human well-being? How will these per capita declines affect efforts to reduce hunger? How long can living standards continue to rise if per capita production of these basic commodities is declining? These questions are troubling ones. They suggest that in many national capitals, food security may replace military security as the principal preoccupation of governments during this decade.

As the per capita supply of basic foodstuffs tightens, it will force both national governments and the international community to focus on the question of distribution. As long as the pie is expanding rapidly and nearly everyone's situation is improving, at least modestly, the distribution question can be avoided. But once the pie is no longer growing quickly or, as could be the case with the fish catch, is not growing at all, then the question of how the pie is sliced becomes a central political issue.

If production of basic foodstuffs such as grain and seafood can no longer match the growth of world population, it raises new philosophical and moral issues. It means that the needs of the 90 million or more people being added each year are being satisfied partly at the expense of those already on the planet. For national governments and the international community, this may lead to a reassessment of population policies.

## DIVERGING ENERGY TRENDS

Among the fossil fuels, striking gains have come in the production of natural gas. (See pages 46–47.) While production of oil has been essentially stagnating for more than a decade, that of natural gas has increased 39 percent during the last eight years. The desire for a cleaner-burning fuel in large urban and industrial centers is partly responsible. For example, several coal-fired

power plants in the United Kingdom have been converted to natural gas. Istanbul, Turkey, a city with serious air pollution, is converting both its power plants and its residences from coal to natural gas.

Attractive prices have also encouraged the global surge in natural gas use. On the supply side, more and more companies and governments have begun to systematically explore for natural gas rather than rely on discoveries that are simply a by-product of oil exploration. Natural gas is also attracting attention as a potential transition fuel, bridging the shift from a fossil-fuel-based economy to one based on solar energy and hydrogen. The infrastructure used to transport and store natural gas can be easily adapted to hydrogen.

Although additional Saudi oil largely compensated for the Gulf War disruption of production in Iraq and Kuwait, world oil production fell 1 percent in 1991, leaving output more than 6 percent below the historical peak reached in 1979. (See pages 44–45.) Among the big three producers—the former Soviet Union, the United States and Saudi Arabia—output is now falling in the first two and is likely to continue doing so for the foreseeable future.

Among the most dramatic political developments on energy is the growing public resistance to nuclear reactors. New plant starts, which numbered 30-50 per year in the seventies and early eighties, dropped to zero in 1990 and to three in 1991. (See pages 48–49.) The industry has been brought to its knees by the high cost of construction and operation, high prospective costs associated with decommissioning worn-out plants, the seemingly insoluble problem of safe disposal of nuclear waste, and links between nuclear power and the spread of nuclear weapons.

One consequence of these recent plant construction trends, combined with worn-out or unsafe plants being closed (as is the case with many in Eastern Europe and the Commonwealth of Independent States), is that growth in nuclear-generated electricity has slowed dramatically. Indeed, in 1991, nuclear generating capacity actually declined for the first time since the nuclear age began.

Dramatic gains in wind-generated electricity and steady growth in sales of photovoltaic cells provide early promise of a far greater role for these environmentally benign renewable energy sources in the future. In California, which has some 1,600 megawatts of wind electric-generation capacity, this source supplies enough electricity to serve the residential needs of nearly a million residents. (See pages 50–51.) Although many still think of wind power as a fad, Wall Street investors have pumped several hundred million dollars into wind turbine manufacturing and wind farms in California alone.

As the cost of photovoltaic cells declines, they are becoming competitive in more and more uses. (See pages 52–53.) Initially economical only to provide electricity on earth-orbiting communication satellites, they have now taken over most of the world market for pocket calculators, replacing batteries. Larger-scale uses include electricity generation in remote regions that are not linked to central grids. Already it is cheaper in many Third World villages to install a local photovoltaic array than it is to build the power lines needed to link these villages to a distant central generating system.

The most serious environmental consequence of fossil fuel use is the emission of carbon dioxide, the principal greenhouse gas that is driving global warming. (See pages 60–61.) Although emissions rose only slightly in 1990 and 1991, scientists believe great cuts are needed to stabilize the global climate. Indeed, since 1959 the carbon dioxide content of the atmosphere has risen by 13 percent, largely as a result of burning fossil fuels.

If this buildup continues as projected, it will lead to a world far warmer than at any time since agriculture began. Average global temperatures have been rising since the mid-sixties, with four of the five warmest years on record occurring during the last five years. (See pages 58–59.) If temperatures keep rising in response to the continued use of fossil fuels, as global meteorological models suggest they will, pressures to boost energy efficiency and shift to renewable energy sources are certain to intensify.

## SOCIAL TRENDS

In the social arena, there are some encouraging trends, but others that are cause for concern. The annual growth in world population set a new record in 1991, at 92 million. (See pages 76–77.) Of this total, 84 million were added in the Third World, in countries already struggling to make ends meet.

Infant mortality rates continue to decline, albeit much more slowly than in previous years. (See pages 78–79.) Efforts by Third World governments, spurred by UNICEF leadership, have greatly reduced infant mortality over the last decade. Immunization of infants for measles and whooping cough and the widespread use of simple oral rehydration therapy to combat dehydration from diarrhea are among the keys to this decline.

While public attention focuses on infant mortality as a prime indicator of changes in a society's health, there is growing evidence that maternal mortality is in some ways an even more sensitive indicator. (See pages 112–13.) Infant mortality in the Third World is some nine times higher than that in the industrial world, but maternal morality is often 100 times as great. In northern Europe, the lifetime risk of a woman dying from pregnancy-related causes is roughly 1 in 10,000. In Africa, it is 1 in 21.

Closely related to trends in infant and maternal mortality is the distribution of income within and among societies. (See pages 110–11.) In many, it has worsened during the last decade or so. In some countries, the incomes of the richest one fifth are 15 times those of the poorest one fifth. In Mexico, the ratio is 18 to 1, and in Brazil it is a staggering 28 to 1. China has the lowest ratio of any country, at 3 to 1. Japan and West Germany, two of the world's most competitive countries, have ratios of 4 to 1 and 5 to 1, respectively. For the world as a whole, the ratio between those living in the wealthiest one fifth of countries and the poorest one fifth is 15 to 1.

During the past four decades, the world has faced some serious threats, notably that of nuclear war. That danger still exists, but it is now diminishing. Even as this is occurring, the formidable new challenges that are emerging, such as the need to stabilize climate and population, will test the capacity of our social institutions. Some, such as the distribution of food in a world where it grows ever more scarce among the poor, will test our humanity as well.

Part **ONE**

# Key Indicators

# Food
## Trends

# Grain Harvest Drops Lester R. Brown

The 1991 world grain harvest fell 84 million tons from the bumper 1990 harvest, the largest one-year drop on record. (See Figure 1.) At 1,696 million tons, it dropped nearly 5 percent in total and, taking into account population growth, 6.4 percent per person.[1] (See Figure 2.)

Between 1950 and 1984, when grain production per person peaked, world output expanded nearly 3 percent a year. During the next seven years, annual growth averaged roughly 1 percent, compared with 1.7 percent for population.[2] With each passing year, the evidence more strongly suggests that weather fluctuations and the drawdown of excessive grain stocks from the mid-eighties may have obscured the transition from an era when grain output expanded much faster than population to one in which the reverse is true.

Just as weather was the key to the record 1990 harvest, it was also largely responsible for the decline in 1991. The reduction in output was concentrated in the former Soviet Union, the world's number three grain producer, and in the United States, which now ranks second, close behind China.[3]

In the United States, a summer of high temperatures combined with areas of drought in the wheat-growing plains and parts of the Corn Belt to reduce the 1991 harvest, marking the fourth time in 12 years that higher temperatures have seriously damaged the U.S. grain harvest.[4]

In the former Soviet Union, sparse rainfall and above-average temperatures in the New Lands area of Kazakhstan and parts of Russia and the Ukraine, particularly the Volga River valley, sharply depressed grain harvests. A decline in deliveries of machinery and spare parts, as well as fuel shortages, also undermined planting schedules and harvesting.[5]

Before the breakup of the Soviet Union, economic reforms that included a shift to world market prices for fertilizer beginning in 1988 doubled the cost of this agricultural input, launching a downward trend in its use. This, combined with energy shortages that reduced nitrogen fertilizer production in 1991, dropped fertilizer use 27 percent from the high in 1987. Some land that is normally fertilized got none at all in 1991.[6]

Although weather largely caused the drop from 1990, the longer-term world food prospect is darkened by several agronomic and environmental trends. Agronomically, the slowdown since 1984 coincided roughly with a cessation in the historical expansion of cropland, a new trend of shrinking irrigated area per person, and a dramatic slowdown in the growth of fertilizer use.

The global cropland area stopped growing during the eighties as gains from plowing new cropland here and there was offset by losses to urbanization and degradation.[7] Even if the United States started producing grain again on cropland under government commodity supply-management programs and on the highly erodible land that was carefully set aside in the Conservation Reserve Program, the world grain area would still not equal that of the early eighties.[8]

Meanwhile, the number of irrigation projects completed each year has declined, resulting in a decrease in irrigated cropland per capita. After expanding by nearly one third between 1950 and 1978, irrigated area per person has shrunk 6 percent since then.[9]

Slower growth in world fertilizer use since 1984 also helps explain the slower growth in the world grain harvest. Between 1950 and 1984, world fertilizer use climbed from 14 to 129 million tons, increasing nearly 7 percent a year. Since 1984, it has expanded an average of less than 2 percent annually.[10] For more than three decades, rapidly expanding fertilizer use was the engine driving the growth in world food output, but that engine is now sputtering. The key question is, Can the 3-percent annual growth in grain output that prevailed from mid-century to 1984 be restored?

Although weather can lead to short-term reductions in food output, environmental degradation is affecting the long-term rate of growth. Research plots and occasional national assessments indicate that soil erosion, air pollution, acid rain, stratospheric ozone depletion, and hotter summers in key grain-growing regions are taking their toll on grain production.[11]

### WORLD GRAIN PRODUCTION, 1950–91

| YEAR | TOTAL (mil. met. tons) | PER CAPITA (kilograms) |
| --- | --- | --- |
| 1950 | 631 | 246 |
| 1951 | 645 | 248 |
| 1952 | 704 | 266 |
| 1953 | 717 | 266 |
| 1954 | 709 | 259 |
| 1955 | 759 | 272 |
| 1956 | 794 | 279 |
| 1957 | 784 | 271 |
| 1958 | 849 | 287 |
| 1959 | 834 | 277 |
| 1960 | 847 | 278 |
| 1961 | 822 | 266 |
| 1962 | 864 | 274 |
| 1963 | 865 | 269 |
| 1964 | 921 | 280 |
| 1965 | 917 | 273 |
| 1966 | 1,005 | 293 |
| 1967 | 1,029 | 294 |
| 1968 | 1,069 | 299 |
| 1969 | 1,078 | 296 |
| 1970 | 1,096 | 295 |
| 1971 | 1,194 | 314 |
| 1972 | 1,156 | 298 |
| 1973 | 1,272 | 322 |
| 1974 | 1,220 | 303 |
| 1975 | 1,250 | 304 |
| 1976 | 1,363 | 326 |
| 1977 | 1,337 | 315 |
| 1978 | 1,467 | 339 |
| 1979 | 1,428 | 325 |
| 1980 | 1,447 | 323 |
| 1981 | 1,499 | 329 |
| 1982 | 1,550 | 334 |
| 1983 | 1,486 | 315 |
| 1984 | 1,649 | 344 |
| 1985 | 1,664 | 341 |
| 1986 | 1,683 | 339 |
| 1987 | 1,612 | 319 |
| 1988 | 1,564 | 304 |
| 1989 | 1,685 | 322 |
| 1990 | 1,780 | 335 |
| 1991 (est) | 1,696 | 314 |

SOURCES: USDA, *World Grain Database* (unpublished printouts) (Washington, D.C.: 1991); USDA, *World Population by Country and Region, 1990.*

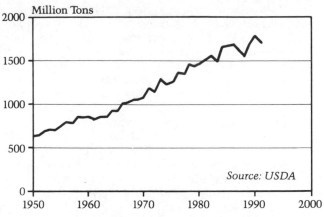

**Figure 1: World Grain Production, 1950–91**

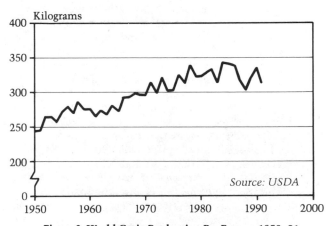

**Figure 2: World Grain Production Per Person, 1950–91**

# Soybean Production Up Lester R. Brown

World soybean production in 1991 was up nearly 2 percent from 1990.[1] (See Figure 1.) Soybean acreage in the United States, which produces over half the world crop, increased somewhat over the preceding year as late spring rains in parts of the Midwest forced farmers to switch from corn to soybeans, which have a shorter maturation period.

Worldwide soybean production slowed dramatically since reaching the all-time per capita high of 21 kilograms in 1979. Between 1950 and 1980, output grew by more than 5 percent annually, but over the last decade growth has averaged only 2 percent a year, barely keeping pace with population.

Following World War II, world soybean production grew by leaps and bounds, increasing from 18 million tons in 1950 to 106 million tons in 1991—nearly a sixfold rise.[2] In the United States, soybeans now rival wheat and corn in the area of cropland they occupy and the income they generate.[3] They are also a leading export earner, ranking with such items as telecommunications equipment and pharmaceuticals.[4]

This enormous growth in output of what is now the world's leading protein crop was fueled by the growing affluence of the postwar decades and the associated growth in consumer demand for livestock products: meat, milk, cheese, poultry, and eggs. In order to use grain efficiently, livestock and poultry need enough protein in their rations to be healthy and well nourished. For many, this comes from soybean meal. After the beans are crushed and the oil extracted, the remaining meal, high in protein, is an ideal supplement to grains in livestock feeds.

Originally domesticated in China, the soybean was traditionally grown as a food crop. Rich in oil, it was a favorite source of cooking oil and was also fermented into bean curd, the "Oriental cheese," a common ingredient in Chinese cuisine. As the surging demand for protein supplements in pork and poultry rations gained momentum in the fifties, the price of the meal rose to the point where it became the principal product, making the oil a by-product.

As recently as 1950, soybeans were still something of a novelty crop in the United States. The four decades since then have witnessed phenomenal growth in U.S. output and the spread of the crop to temperate-zone Latin America, where Brazil, Argentina, and Paraguay together produce one third of the world harvest.

In 1950, China was the leading soybean producer, accounting for two thirds of the world harvest. Its 1991 soybean harvest, however, at 10 million tons, was little changed from the 1950 level. With one tenth of the global total, China ranked third, behind the United States and Brazil.[5]

As incomes rise in low-income countries, consumption of vegetable oil for cooking and of livestock products, particularly poultry and pork, also increases, generating ever greater demand for soybeans. From 1950 until the bumper harvest of 1979, when per capita soybean output peaked, the world harvest grew over 4 percent a year, tracking the rise in affluence. After climbing from 7 kilograms to 21 kilograms during this 29-year span, per capita production has levelled off.[6] (See Figure 2.) Vast numbers of people in the world would consume more protein and use more vegetable oil if they could afford it.

Future growth in soybean production may not come as easily. The growth comes largely from expanding the area planted, which has nearly tripled since 1950 while yield per hectare has risen less than two thirds.[7] Yields have risen slowly because soybeans, as legumes, fix their own nitrogen, and are therefore not as responsive to nitrogen fertilizer as grain crops are.

With the heavy dependence on more land to boost soybean output and with new land becoming scarce, farmers may not be able to keep pace with population growth much longer. If soybean production per person begins to fall, which is now a distinct possibility unless population growth slows dramatically, it will be far more difficult for the world's poor to obtain the cooking oil and livestock products they want.

## WORLD SOYBEAN PRODUCTION, 1950–91

| YEAR | TOTAL (mill. met. tons) | PER CAPITA (kilograms) |
|------|------|------|
| 1950 | 18 | 7 |
| 1951 | 17 | 7 |
| 1952 | 18 | 7 |
| 1953 | 18 | 7 |
| 1954 | 20 | 7 |
| 1955 | 21 | 7 |
| 1956 | 24 | 8 |
| 1957 | 25 | 9 |
| 1958 | 28 | 10 |
| 1959 | 28 | 9 |
| 1960 | 27 | 9 |
| 1961 | 31 | 10 |
| 1962 | 31 | 10 |
| 1963 | 32 | 10 |
| 1964 | 32 | 10 |
| 1965 | 37 | 11 |
| 1966 | 39 | 11 |
| 1967 | 41 | 12 |
| 1968 | 44 | 12 |
| 1969 | 45 | 12 |
| 1970 | 46 | 12 |
| 1971 | 48 | 13 |
| 1972 | 49 | 13 |
| 1973 | 62 | 16 |
| 1974 | 55 | 14 |
| 1975 | 66 | 16 |
| 1976 | 59 | 14 |
| 1977 | 72 | 17 |
| 1978 | 78 | 18 |
| 1979 | 94 | 21 |
| 1980 | 81 | 18 |
| 1981 | 86 | 19 |
| 1982 | 94 | 20 |
| 1983 | 83 | 18 |
| 1984 | 93 | 19 |
| 1985 | 97 | 20 |
| 1986 | 98 | 20 |
| 1987 | 104 | 21 |
| 1988 | 96 | 19 |
| 1989 | 107 | 20 |
| 1990 | 104 | 20 |
| 1991 | 106 | 20 |

SOURCE: USDA, *World Oilseed Database*
(unpublished printouts) (Washington, D.C.: 1991).

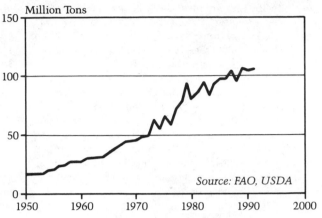

**Figure 1: World Soybean Production, 1950–91**

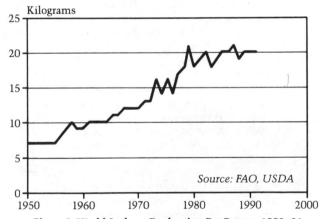

**Figure 2: World Soybean Production Per Person, 1950–91**

# Meat Production Rises                    Lester R. Brown

In 1991, world meat production of all kinds—beef, mutton, pork, and poultry—reached nearly 173 million tons, a rise from just over 171 million tons in 1990.[1] (See Figure 1.) The fourfold growth in meat production since 1950 closely parallels the expansion of the world economy, a trend driven by both population increase and rising affluence.[2] In the Third World, the drive for larger herds and flocks is the result of demographic growth, which has tripled the populations of many countries since mid-century.[3] In North America, Europe, and East Asia, the enormous increase in demand is largely a response to rising incomes.

Worldwide, production per person climbed from 18 kilograms in 1950 to 32 kilograms in 1986, where it has remained for the last six years.[4] (See Figure 2.) In part, this levelling off is due to the deterioration of rangelands from overgrazing, a process that afflicts both industrial and developing countries. For example, a 1987 survey of U.S. grazing lands managed by the Bureau of Land Management showed 30 percent to be in good condition and 58 percent to be fair or poor condition.[5] A U.N. survey reported that in nine countries of Southern Africa, "present herds exceed the carrying capacity by 50 to 100 percent."[6]

Since 1984, declining per capita production of grain has restricted the amount available for livestock and poultry.[7] Slower growth in output of soybeans, the principal protein supplement used in livestock rations, may also be a factor.[8] And on the demand side, slower economic growth in many middle- and lower-income countries is discouraging the consumption of more meat.

Cattle, sheep, and goats are ruminants—animals with four stomachs. This complex digestive system enables them to thrive on roughage, principally grass, which humans cannot eat. Although uniquely able to convert grass into meat, they are not particularly efficient at converting grain into meat. Cattle in the feedlot typically require seven pounds of grain to gain a pound in weight. Pigs, meanwhile, require four pounds of grain, and chickens, scarcely two.[9]

The comparatively slow growth in output of beef since the mid-seventies reflects the constraints imposed by the earth's grazing capacity. Since 1950, beef production has expanded just 2.7 times, going from 19 million to 52 million tons.[10] (See Figure 3.) Growth in mutton production, including both sheep and goats, has been even slower, scarcely doubling.[11] These animals are concentrated in semiarid regions, such as North Africa, the Middle East, and Australia, that typically suffer from extensive overgrazing.

The parallel growth in beef and pork production ended in the late seventies as expanding cattle herds pressed against grazing limits, slowing their growth.[12] Meanwhile, in China, agricultural reforms dramatically boosted grain production, leading to a surge in pork production that pushed world output far above beef, making it the leading meat.[13]

By far the greatest growth in meat production has been in poultry, principally chickens and to a lesser degree turkeys and ducks, which has increased ninefold since 1950.[14] This growth has come from advances in production technology, including the development of rapidly maturing breeds that are highly efficient in converting grain to meat. While rising affluence was driving meat consumption upward, emerging concerns with diets overly rich in fat were leading consumers to leaner beef and pork and to poultry and fish.

Meat consumption varies widely among countries, ranging from 112 kilograms per person annually in the United States to only 2 kilograms in India. Australia trails closely behind the United States, with 104 kilograms per year. In France and Germany, consumption averages about 90 kilograms; in Brazil, Japan, and Mexico, it ranges from 40 to 47 kilograms. China's 1.2 billion people, further down the income ladder, eat an average of 24 kilograms each.[15]

With additional output of beef and mutton now heavily dependent on expanded supplies of grain and soybeans, the levelling off in per capita meat production should come as no surprise. At issue is whether adding more than 90 million people a year during the nineties will overwhelm meat production expansion efforts and trigger a long-term decline in meat consumption per person.

WORLD MEAT PRODUCTION, 1950–91

| YEAR | TOTAL (mill. met. tons) | PER CAPITA (kilograms) |
|------|------|------|
| 1950 | 46 | 18 |
| 1951 | 50 | 19 |
| 1952 | 53 | 20 |
| 1953 | 56 | 21 |
| 1954 | 58 | 22 |
| 1955 | 60 | 22 |
| 1956 | 63 | 22 |
| 1957 | 65 | 23 |
| 1958 | 67 | 23 |
| 1959 | 69 | 23 |
| 1960 | 68 | 22 |
| 1961 | 70 | 23 |
| 1962 | 73 | 23 |
| 1963 | 77 | 24 |
| 1964 | 78 | 24 |
| 1965 | 82 | 25 |
| 1966 | 86 | 25 |
| 1967 | 90 | 26 |
| 1968 | 93 | 26 |
| 1969 | 94 | 26 |
| 1970 | 98 | 26 |
| 1971 | 102 | 27 |
| 1972 | 105 | 27 |
| 1973 | 106 | 27 |
| 1974 | 112 | 28 |
| 1975 | 113 | 28 |
| 1976 | 116 | 28 |
| 1977 | 120 | 28 |
| 1978 | 125 | 29 |
| 1979 | 129 | 30 |
| 1980 | 133 | 30 |
| 1981 | 136 | 30 |
| 1982 | 137 | 30 |
| 1983 | 142 | 30 |
| 1984 | 145 | 30 |
| 1985 | 150 | 31 |
| 1986 | 156 | 32 |
| 1987 | 161 | 32 |
| 1988 | 164 | 32 |
| 1989 | 167 | 32 |
| 1990 | 171 | 32 |
| 1991 | 173 | 32 |

SOURCES: FAO, *1948–1985 World Crop and Livestock Statistics* (Rome: 1987); FAO, *FAO Production Yearbooks 1988–1991*; USDA, *World Agricultural Production,* August and September 1991; Worldwatch estimates.

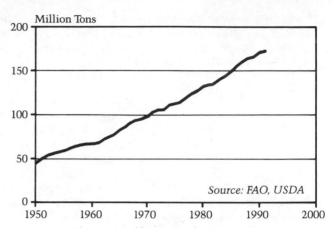

Figure 1: World Meat Production, 1950–91

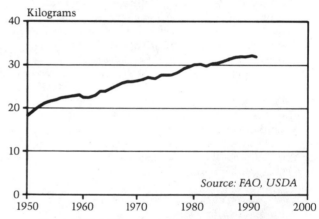

Figure 2: World Meat Production Per Person, 1950–91

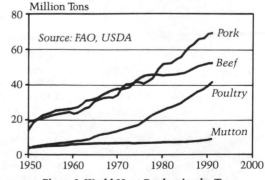

Figure 3: World Meat Production by Type, 1950–91

29

# Fish Catch Falls                                                Hal Kane

In 1990, the world fish catch fell to 97 million tons, down from a record 100 million tons the preceding year.[1] (See Figure 1.) The marine biologists of the U.N. Food and Agriculture Organization (FAO) who monitor fish catches think that 100 million tons is the maximum annual harvest that the oceans can sustain.[2] Part of the drop was due to trends in the former Soviet Union, where the catch fell from 11.3 million tons in 1989 to 10.4 million in 1990,[3] and part was due to a reduction in fish stocks stemming from earlier overharvesting of some species.

Growth in the world fish catch from 22 million tons in 1950 to the all-time high of 100 million tons was not always smooth. After slowing dramatically during the seventies, rapid growth was restored during the late eighties as larger-yielding fishing techniques, including the use of driftnets, were adopted and as the harvest of less desirable species expanded. Some 70 percent of the steep rise since 1982 is from increased landings of Peruvian anchovy, South American sardine, Japanese sardine, and the Alaskan Pollock.[4] Some of the remainder came from exploitation of untapped fish stocks in more remote areas of the southern Pacific.

Today, overfishing threatens many commercially important fish species. Catches of Atlantic cod, haddock, Atlantic herring, capelin, Southern African pilchard, Pacific Ocean perch, King Crab, and the Peruvian anchoveta have all declined from overfishing.[5] If overfishing continues to deplete stocks, it will threaten not only those who depend on seafood for protein, but more than 100 million people who depend on the oceans for their livelihood as well.[6]

To compensate for losses among species with falling stocks, fishers have intensified pressures on other species. Aquaculture is also picking up some of the slack: In 1988, the world's fish farmers produced 14.5 million tons of fish, up nearly 40 percent from the 1984 harvest of 10.5 million tons.[7]

Although fish account for only 16 percent of the animal-protein supply for the world as a whole, they provide as much as 40 percent in some developing countries.[8] For a few industrial countries, such as Norway and Japan, fish are the dominant source of animal protein. Rapidly escalating world demand has caused the price of seafood to more than double in real terms in the United States since the mid-sixties, while prices of beef and pork have held constant and that of chicken has declined.[9]

Fish stocks are also suffering from the destruction of habitats and breeding grounds by coastal development, nutrient contamination of offshore waters from industrial effluents, agricultural run-off, ocean dumping, and litter. Some fisheries are no longer harvested because their chemically contaminated produce is unsafe for human consumption.

Stratospheric ozone depletion may disrupt marine ecosystems, as too much ultraviolet radiation slows the reproduction and photosynthetic efficiency of phytoplankton, eroding the foundation of the oceanic food chain. Similarly, rising ocean water temperatures due to the greenhouse effect may also upset marine habitats.

Efforts to protect fish yields have often concentrated on stronger national laws and management of fish stocks. In 1982, for example, national economic boundaries were extended to 200 miles from the shoreline—an area that yields more than 90 percent of the ocean's fish catch. This, it was hoped, would give countries a stake in carefully managing their fish stocks to maximize sustainable yields.

Although this has helped in numerous instances, many developing nations lack naval patrols to enforce stringent controls on fishing. In addition, fish stocks migrate among the waters of different countries. Canada, for example, has had a particularly hard time protecting its endangered yields of Atlantic cod because of unrestrained exploitation of that species when it migrates to other waters.[10]

After more than doubling from 9 kilograms in 1950 to 19 kilograms in 1989, the world fish catch per person dropped nearly 5 percent in 1990.[11] (See Figure 2.) If FAO estimates of a sustainable world catch of 100 million tons are reasonable, then continuing population growth will lead to a steady decline in per capita ocean harvesting. If seafood prices continue to rise, the world's poor may be affected most of all.

## WORLD FISH CATCH, 1950–90

| YEAR | TOTAL (mill. met. tons) | PER CAPITA (kilograms) |
|---|---|---|
| 1950 | 22 | 9 |
| 1951 | 26 | 10 |
| 1952 | 25 | 10 |
| 1953 | 26 | 10 |
| 1954 | 27 | 10 |
| 1955 | 29 | 10 |
| 1956 | 30 | 11 |
| 1957 | 31 | 11 |
| 1958 | 33 | 11 |
| 1959 | 36 | 12 |
| 1960 | 38 | 12 |
| 1961 | 42 | 14 |
| 1962 | 45 | 14 |
| 1963 | 48 | 15 |
| 1964 | 53 | 16 |
| 1965 | 54 | 16 |
| 1966 | 57 | 17 |
| 1967 | 60 | 17 |
| 1968 | 64 | 18 |
| 1969 | 63 | 17 |
| 1970 | 66 | 18 |
| 1971 | 66 | 17 |
| 1972 | 62 | 16 |
| 1973 | 63 | 16 |
| 1974 | 67 | 16 |
| 1975 | 66 | 16 |
| 1976 | 69 | 17 |
| 1977 | 70 | 16 |
| 1978 | 70 | 16 |
| 1979 | 71 | 16 |
| 1980 | 72 | 16 |
| 1981 | 75 | 16 |
| 1982 | 77 | 17 |
| 1983 | 78 | 16 |
| 1984 | 84 | 17 |
| 1985 | 86 | 18 |
| 1986 | 92 | 19 |
| 1987 | 93 | 18 |
| 1988 | 99 | 19 |
| 1989 | 100 | 19 |
| 1990 (est) | 97 | 18 |

SOURCE: FAO, *FAO Production Yearbook: Fishery Statistics, Commodities* (Rome: various years).

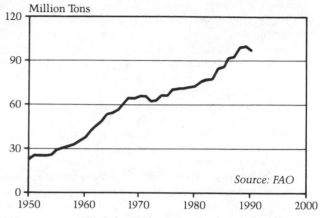

**Figure 1: World Fish Catch, 1950–90**

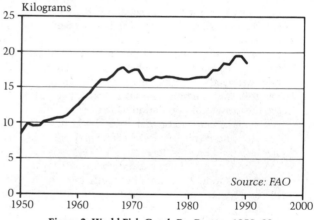

**Figure 2: World Fish Catch Per Person, 1950–90**

# Grain Stocks Decline                    Lester R. Brown

When the 1992 harvest began, grain stocks to-talled an estimated 310 million tons, down from 337 million tons in 1991. (See Figure 1.) Amounting to only 66 days of world consumption, reserves were among the lowest in years.[1] (See Figure 2.)

World carryover stocks of grain—the amount in the bin when the new harvest begins—are a key indicator of food security for the world's 5.4 billion people. Whenever stocks drop, it means that consumption for the year just ended exceeded production.

Carryover stocks of grain are an important indicator of food security for two reasons. First, grain consumed directly supplies half of human food energy intake, and it supplies part of the remainder when consumed indirectly in the form of meat, milk, eggs, cheese, and butter. Second, because they are less perishable than most fruits and vegetables, grains can be stored to supply food during the winter season in the higher latitudes and during the dry season in areas with monsoonal climates.

With world grain production in 1991 down 84 million tons from the year before, stocks would have dropped even more if world consumption had followed the normal upward trend, paralleling the growth of population. However, consumption appears to have dropped by 17 million tons.[2] Without this belt-tightening, carryover stocks would be even lower.

When world grain stocks drop below 60 days of consumption, they amount to little more than the basic minimum needed to keep supply lines operating. In the modern world, where consumers and producers are widely separated, large quantities of grain are required just to keep the pipeline between the two filled. Wheat moving from U.S. farms to Russian consumers, for example, passes through a grain elevator on a wheat farm in the Great Plains, a train, a portside elevator, a ship, a portside elevator in Russia, a train to an elevator at a flour mill, and a truck to a bakery; finally, the bread must then be distributed in the community where it will be consumed. An interruption anywhere along this supply line can disrupt consumption.

At 60 days' worth of grain stocks, an adverse weather report from a major food-growing region anywhere can send prices soaring. In 1973, when world grain stocks dropped to 55 days of consumption, grain prices doubled, creating unprecedented instability in the world food economy.[3]

Following a poor harvest, such as the drought-induced shortfall in South Africa, Zimbabwe, and Zambia in 1992, countries quickly exhaust their grain stocks and must depend on imported grain to avoid famine.[4] If exporting countries such as the United States were not holding large stocks, millions would die before the next harvest.

The food situation in 1992 is particularly difficult because of the breakup of the Soviet Union, which has disrupted the highly centralized, Moscow-centered food procurement and distribution system. This, coupled with short-term disruptions from the privatization of agriculture in Russia and several other states in the new Commonwealth, could lead to food shortages.

In addition to its carryover stocks, the world has a second line of defense against food shortages—the cropland idled under commodity supply-management programs in countries where farm support prices generate more output than the market and food aid programs will absorb. Most of this land is in the United States, where in 1991 some 5 million hectares (less than 1 percent of world grain area) were set aside.[5] An additional 14 million hectares of highly erodible U.S. cropland has been planted to grass or trees since early 1986 under the Conservation Reserve Program, but it would be unwise to disturb that.[6]

A third reserve is the grain fed to livestock and poultry, an amount in excess of 600 million tons yearly, roughly one third of the harvest.[7] Although all grains fed to livestock are also widely consumed for food, this reserve is far more difficult to tap. A substantial rise in grain prices would reduce the amount fed to livestock, but at this price level the world's poorest people could not buy enough grain to survive. Alternatively, affluent-society governments could free up grain for human consumption by rationing the sale of livestock products, but this is politically difficult, to say the least.

WORLD GRAIN ENDING STOCKS, 1962–91

| YEAR | STOCKS (mill. met. tons) | CONSUMPTION (days) |
|------|------|------|
| 1962 | 190 | 81 |
| 1963 | 193 | 82 |
| 1964 | 194 | 77 |
| 1965 | 159 | 61 |
| 1966 | 190 | 71 |
| 1967 | 213 | 77 |
| 1968 | 244 | 86 |
| 1969 | 228 | 76 |
| 1970 | 193 | 62 |
| 1971 | 217 | 68 |
| 1972 | 180 | 55 |
| 1973 | 192 | 56 |
| 1974 | 200 | 60 |
| 1975 | 220 | 65 |
| 1976 | 280 | 78 |
| 1977 | 279 | 76 |
| 1978 | 328 | 84 |
| 1979 | 316 | 80 |
| 1980 | 288 | 71 |
| 1981 | 308 | 76 |
| 1982 | 357 | 87 |
| 1983 | 304 | 72 |
| 1984 | 365 | 84 |
| 1985 | 433 | 99 |
| 1986 | 463 | 102 |
| 1987 | 408 | 89 |
| 1988 | 316 | 70 |
| 1989 | 300 | 64 |
| 1990 (prel) | 337 | 71 |
| 1991 (est) | 310 | 66 |

SOURCE: USDA, *World Grain Situation and Outlook*, April 1992.

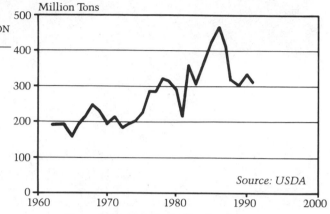

Figure 1: World Grain Ending Stocks, 1962–91

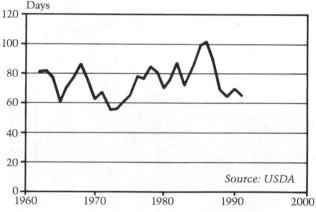

Figure 2: World Grain Ending Stocks as
Days of Consumption, 1962–91

# Agricultural Resource
# Trends

# Grainland Shrinks

Lester R. Brown

In 1991, the world's harvested area of grain shrank from 695 million hectares to 693 million, a drop of 0.3 percent.[1] (See Figure 1.) This drop, combined with the addition of 92 million people to the earth's population, led to a reduction of 2.0 percent in grain area per person, adding to a decline that has been under way since mid-century.[2] (See Figure 2.)

Historically, the population-land relationship divides neatly into three periods. From the beginning of agriculture until 1950, nearly all the growth in world food output came from expanding cultivated area. From 1950 to 1980, roughly four fifths came from raising land productivity. Since then, all the increases in output have come from raising land productivity, since the grain area has not expanded at all.[3] With no meaningful expansion in prospect during the nineties, future growth in world grain output can come only from raising land productivity.

There are still occasional increases in cropland area here and there. Brazil, for example, more than doubled its area in grain between 1960 and 1980. Since then, however, the area has not expanded.[4] A few countries are raising grain-harvested area by multiple cropping—combining, for example, winter wheat with a summer rice crop.[5] On balance, however, these gains are offset by losses as cropland is converted to nonfarm uses or abandoned because of severe degradation.

The impact of shifting land to nonfarm uses is most pronounced in China, which is losing almost 1 million hectares a year, nearly 1 percent of its cropland.[6] One result of the prosperity since economic reforms were launched in 1976 is that literally millions of villagers are either expanding their houses or building new ones.[7] And an average annual industrial growth rate of 8.6 percent since 1980 means the construction of thousands of new factories.[8] Since most of China's 1.1 billion people are concentrated in its rich farming regions, new homes and factories are often built on cropland. This loss, combined with a shift to more profitable crops, has reduced the grain harvested area in China by roughly one tenth from its historical peak in 1976.[9]

Urban sprawl is also claiming cropland. In Thailand, the expansion of Bangkok, driven by both prosperity and population growth, has claimed an average of 3,200 hectares each year during the past decade.[10] Similarly, in Egypt, new building invariably comes at the expense of cropland, since the nation's 54 million people live on the thin ribbon of irrigated cropland along the Nile River.[11]

Another leading source of cropland loss is degradation from erosion. In countless abandoned villages in Ethiopia, for example, there is not enough soil left to support even subsistence-level agriculture. And in the former Soviet Union, land degradation, mostly from soil erosion, helped reduce the area in grain 20 percent between its 1977 peak and 1991.[12]

In the United States, the Conservation Reserve Program is designed to convert highly erodible cropland to either grassland or woodland before it loses its productivity. Since 1985, this has taken 14 million hectares, roughly one tenth of all cropland, out of production.[13] Lacking such a program, many other countries have simply continued to farm land until erosion converts it to wasteland.

Cropland is also being lost indirectly through the growing diversion of irrigation water to cities in desert areas. Arizona has purchased the irrigation rights to large areas of cropland and converted them back to desert in order to consume the water in its cities.[14] Yet another source of cropland loss is nuclear irradiation, most of it in the Ukraine and Belarus. As a result of the 1986 Chernobyl explosion, at least a half-million hectares of cropland have been lost as communities no longer safe for human habitation were abandoned.[15]

On balance, efforts to expand cropland are offset by losses. As a result, the world's grainland area has not expanded for the past decade—nor is it likely to during the nineties. With the continuing addition of some 90 million or more people each year over the rest of this decade, the amount of cropland per person will shrink accordingly.

## WORLD GRAIN HARVESTED AREA, 1950–91

| YEAR | TOTAL (mill. hectares) |
|------|------------------------|
| 1950 | 593 |
| 1951 | 595 |
| 1952 | 615 |
| 1953 | 626 |
| 1954 | 634 |
| 1955 | 646 |
| 1956 | 655 |
| 1957 | 651 |
| 1958 | 653 |
| 1959 | 642 |
| 1960 | 651 |
| 1961 | 647 |
| 1962 | 655 |
| 1963 | 660 |
| 1964 | 660 |
| 1965 | 657 |
| 1966 | 659 |
| 1967 | 669 |
| 1968 | 674 |
| 1969 | 675 |
| 1970 | 666 |
| 1971 | 675 |
| 1972 | 664 |
| 1973 | 691 |
| 1974 | 693 |
| 1975 | 711 |
| 1976 | 719 |
| 1977 | 716 |
| 1978 | 716 |
| 1979 | 713 |
| 1980 | 724 |
| 1981 | 735 |
| 1982 | 718 |
| 1983 | 709 |
| 1984 | 712 |
| 1985 | 717 |
| 1986 | 711 |
| 1987 | 686 |
| 1988 | 690 |
| 1989 | 696 |
| 1990 | 695 |
| 1991 (prel) | 693 |

SOURCE: USDA, *World Grain Database* (unpublished printouts) (Washington, D.C.: 1991).

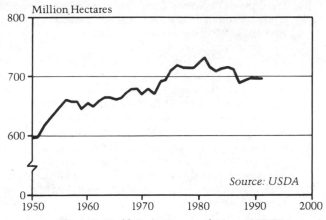

**Figure 1: World Grain Harvested Area, 1950–91**

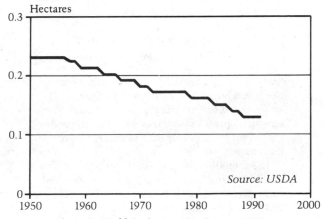

**Figure 2: World Grain Area Per Person, 1950–91**

# Irrigation Expansion Slowing                Lester R. Brown

From the time the first farmers irrigated their fields several thousand years ago in the Middle East until 1950, world irrigated area gradually expanded until it covered 94 million hectares. From 1950 until 1978, when the area per person peaked, the amount of irrigated land more than doubled, climbing to 206 million hectares. During this period, the irrigated area per person increased some 28 percent, or 1 percent a year.[1] Since then, growth has slowed dramatically, reaching 235 million hectares in 1989 for a gain of 14 percent over 11 years. (See Figure 1.) With expansion much slower than that of population, the irrigated area per person shrank 6 percent during this time.[2] (See Figure 2.)

China and India lead the world in irrigated land. In China, this agricultural practice grew impressively between 1950 and 1980, increasing from scarcely 20 million hectares in 1950 to some 48 million by 1980. The growth facilitated an increase in multiple cropping, from an average of 1.3 crops per hectare in 1950 to 1.5 in 1980.[3]

India's net irrigated area, almost exactly the same as China's in 1950, grew less rapidly, reaching some 39 million hectares in 1980. Introduction of the high-yielding wheat and rice varieties that were both more responsive to the use of water and more exacting in their demands greatly enhanced profitability, which stimulated widespread investments by small farmers in wells of their own.[4]

The United States and the former Soviet Union rank third and fourth, respectively, in irrigated area.[5] Growth in U.S. irrigated area from 1950 to 1980 was concentrated in the southern Great Plains.[6] Soviet irrigated area, much of it near the Aral Sea, grew steadily during the same period.[7]

Unfortunately, not all the growth in irrigation is sustainable. In 1986, the U.S. Department of Agriculture (USDA) reported that more than one fifth of the 21 million hectares of U.S. irrigated cropland was being watered by pulling down water tables, with the drop ranging from six inches to four feet per year.[8] Although overpumping is an option in the short run, in the long run withdrawals cannot exceed aquifer recharge.

In China, where the expansion ended in 1978, irrigated area had shrunk 2 percent by 1987. Under parts of the North China Plain, which includes Beijing, the water table is dropping by one meter per year.[9] Overpumping is evident in India as well. Although no groundwater study comparable to the USDA survey has been done there, several states have reported that water tables are falling and wells are going dry.[10]

In the Commonwealth of Independent States, the excessive use of water for irrigation takes the form of diminished river flows rather than falling water tables. Most of the irrigated cropland is in central Asia, much of it watered by the Syr-Darya and Amu-Darya, the two great rivers of the region, both emptying into the Aral Sea. Irrigation diversions from these rivers have greatly reduced their flow into the landlocked Aral, which is now some 40 percent smaller than it was in 1960. As a result, the seabed is becoming desert, the site of sandstorms that each year may drop on the surrounding fields up to a half-ton per hectare of a sand-salt mix—damaging the very crops that water once destined for the sea is used to grow. C.I.S. scientists fear a major ecological catastrophe is unfolding as the sea slowly disappears.[11]

Competition for available freshwater supplies between farmers and city-dwellers is intensifying. In the western United States, state laws make it difficult to buy rights to water independent of the land, so growing cities are buying farmland—solely in order to secure increased water rights.[12] In north China, when water supplies are tight the government on at least one occasion denied water to all farmers except those growing vegetables.[13]

On balance, it now seems unlikely that the rapid growth in world irrigated area will be reestablished. To the extent that the irrigated area does expand in the future, it may depend as much on gains in water use efficiency as on new supplies.[14]

## WORLD IRRIGATED AREA, 1950 AND 1961–89

| YEAR | TOTAL (mill. hectares) | PER CAPITA (hectares per 1,000 pop.) |
|------|------|------|
| 1950 | 94 | 37.4 |
| 1961 | 139 | 45.3 |
| 1962 | 142 | 45.2 |
| 1963 | 145 | 45.2 |
| 1964 | 148 | 45.1 |
| 1965 | 151 | 45.1 |
| 1966 | 154 | 45.2 |
| 1967 | 157 | 45.1 |
| 1968 | 160 | 45.2 |
| 1969 | 165 | 45.5 |
| 1970 | 169 | 45.5 |
| 1971 | 172 | 45.6 |
| 1972 | 176 | 45.7 |
| 1973 | 181 | 46.3 |
| 1974 | 185 | 46.3 |
| 1975 | 191 | 46.7 |
| 1976 | 196 | 47.2 |
| 1977 | 201 | 47.5 |
| 1978 | 206 | 47.9 |
| 1979 | 209 | 47.8 |
| 1980 | 211 | 47.5 |
| 1981 | 215 | 47.4 |
| 1982 | 216 | 46.9 |
| 1983 | 217 | 46.3 |
| 1984 | 223 | 46.8 |
| 1985 | 225 | 46.4 |
| 1986 | 227 | 46.0 |
| 1987 | 228 | 45.3 |
| 1988 | 230 | 45.0 |
| 1989 | 235 | 45.1 |

SOURCES: Worldwatch Institute derived from FAO, *Production Yearbook* (Rome: various years); Bill Quimby, USDA, ERS, private communication, March 20, 1992.

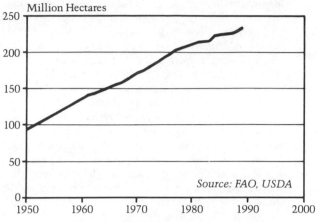

Figure 1: World Irrigated Area, 1950–89

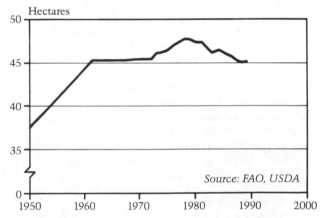

Figure 2: World Irrigated Area Per Thousand People, 1950–89

# Fertilizer Use Falls                    Lester R. Brown

In 1991, the world's farmers used 1 percent less fertilizer than in the previous year. Following on the heels of an even larger drop in 1989, it marked the first consecutive two-year decline on record. From an all-time high of 144 million tons in 1989, world fertilizer use fell to 136 million tons in 1991, a drop of 6 percent.[1] (See Figure 1.)

In the United States, the world's leading food producer, farmers are using less fertilizer than they did a decade ago.[2] (See Figure 2.) Fertilizer use in other agriculturally advanced countries, such as Japan and those in Europe, is growing little if at all. The principal reason for the change is the diminishing response of crop yields to the application of additional fertilizer in many countries, including some in the Third World.[3]

Between 1950 and 1984, when per capita grain production peaked, world fertilizer use climbed from 14 to 129 million tons, multiplying ninefold, or nearly 7 percent per year. Since then, it has expanded at less than 2 percent annually—and growth in grain output has slowed dramatically.[4]

Several trends converged at mid-century to launch the steep climb in world fertilizer use. By then, the frontiers of agricultural settlement had largely disappeared. And, almost overnight, population growth shifted from low gear to high. Faced with record growth in world food demand and little new land to plow, farmers responded by pouring on fertilizer to raise land productivity, boosting their grain yields from 1.1 to 2.4 tons per hectare within four decades.[5]

The breeding of higher yielding strains of corn, wheat, rice, and other cereals that were more responsive to fertilizer went hand in hand with the growth in fertilizer use.[6] So, too, did the doubling of world irrigated area from 1950 to 1980.[7]

Another demographic trend, the massive urbanization since mid-century, disrupted nutrient cycles. The traditional rural recycling of human waste was replaced with urban sewage systems that, more often than not, dumped valuable nutrients into nearby rivers or the sea. This continuous loss forced farmers to add nutrients in mineral or chemical form to preserve land fertility.

Seeing fertilizers as the key to expanding food output, many governments decided to subsidize their use. Today, efforts to rationalize economic activity in many developing countries, often encouraged by the World Bank, have eliminated this practice.[8] In the Soviet Union, the adoption of world market prices raised fertilizer prices sharply, dropping its use by 27 percent from 1988 to 1991 and reducing excessive use.[9]

Worldwide, the trends that spurred the enormous expansion in fertilizer use are changing. For example, growth in the world irrigated area has slowed dramatically since 1980.[10] Similarly, the high-yielding varieties whose rapid spread led to quantum jumps in output are already planted on most of the land that is suitable.

Higher oil prices in late 1990 and 1991 raised fertilizer prices, as did the disruption of fertilizer production in Iraq and Kuwait, both normally exporters. Higher fertilizer prices and relatively low grain prices have discouraged use in some countries.

More important than these short-term economic influences, however, is the diminishing agronomic response of crop yields to fertilizer use. During the sixties, the application of an additional ton of fertilizer in the U.S. Corn Belt could boost output by 20 tons.[11] Today, an additional ton of fertilizer may not raise output by more than one fourth that amount.[12]

Even in some developing countries where grain harvests have risen dramatically over the last two decades, the response to more fertilizer is now muted. In a 1987 analysis of recent trends in Indonesia, Cornell economists Duane Chapman and Randy Barker note that "while one kilogram of fertilizer nutrients probably led to a yield increase of 10 kilograms of unmilled rice in 1972, this ratio has fallen to about one to five at present."[13] In China, growth in use slowed in 1991 and could now start to level off, as it has in the United States.[14] (See Figure 3.)

Some countries—Argentina, India, and Nigeria among them—still have a great deal of latitude to raise fertilizer use.[15] But for the world as a whole, the potential for profitably using more fertilizer has diminished in recent years.

## WORLD FERTILIZER USE, 1950–91

| YEAR | AMOUNT (mill. met. tons) |
|------|--------|
| 1950 | 14 |
| 1951 | 15 |
| 1952 | 15 |
| 1953 | 16 |
| 1954 | 17 |
| 1955 | 18 |
| 1956 | 20 |
| 1957 | 22 |
| 1958 | 23 |
| 1959 | 25 |
| 1960 | 27 |
| 1961 | 28 |
| 1962 | 31 |
| 1963 | 34 |
| 1964 | 37 |
| 1965 | 40 |
| 1966 | 45 |
| 1967 | 51 |
| 1968 | 56 |
| 1969 | 60 |
| 1970 | 66 |
| 1971 | 69 |
| 1972 | 73 |
| 1973 | 79 |
| 1974 | 85 |
| 1975 | 82 |
| 1976 | 90 |
| 1977 | 95 |
| 1978 | 100 |
| 1979 | 111 |
| 1980 | 115 |
| 1981 | 114 |
| 1982 | 114 |
| 1983 | 124 |
| 1984 | 129 |
| 1985 | 129 |
| 1986 | 133 |
| 1987 | 141 |
| 1988 | 144 |
| 1989 | 144 |
| 1990 (prel) | 138 |
| 1991 (est) | 136 |

SOURCE: FAO, The Fertilizer Institute, and Worldwatch Institute.

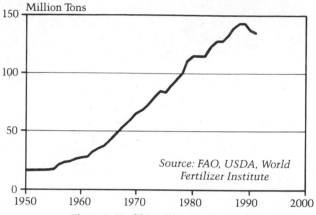

Source: FAO, USDA, World Fertilizer Institute

**Figure 1: World Fertilizer Use, 1950–91**

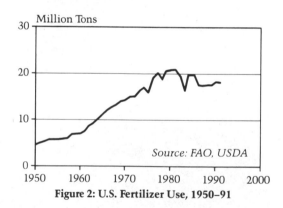

Source: FAO, USDA

**Figure 2: U.S. Fertilizer Use, 1950–91**

Source: USDA

**Figure 3: Fertilizer Use in China, 1950–91**

41

# Energy Trends

# Oil Production Falls Christopher Flavin

World oil production fell 1 percent in 1991—and has still not regained the record set 12 years earlier.[1] (See Figure 1.) At 59 million barrels per day, world oil production in 1991 was 6 percent lower than in 1979. The levelling off of global output is largely a result of lower consumption, mainly in industrial market nations. The oil price increases of the seventies led to far-reaching efficiency improvements and to shifts toward natural gas and coal.

World consumption and production of oil increased steadily from 1950 to 1973, at roughly 7 percent annually.[2] By the seventies, global demand was pressing uncomfortably close to the world's maximum production capacity. The oil crises of 1973 and 1979 led to temporary supply disruptions and sudden price spurts, since there was no quick way to replace the lost oil.

Since 1980, however, the world economy has never been up against the limits of global production. Throughout the past decade, several Middle Eastern nations have deliberately limited production in order to maintain prices. Nonetheless, the unwillingness of the members of the Organization of Petroleum Exporting Countries to cut production indefinitely led to a sharp drop in average prices—from $36 per barrel in 1981 to $13 at the end of 1986.[3] Since then, world petroleum production has been determined mainly by the level of demand, which has slowly rebounded as prices have stabilized at $16-18 per barrel.

During the 1990 Persian Gulf crisis, spot oil prices shot upward briefly, from $16 in July to $35 per barrel in November.[4] Unlike in the seventies, however, this crisis was short-lived—not because of the quick allied victory in the war, but because the world had excess production capacity to draw on. Within a few months, Saudi Arabia was able to make up for 3 million barrels per day of lost Iraqi and Kuwaiti oil exports, bringing oil prices down rapidly.[5]

In the nineties, however, the world oil market may tighten. Output in the United States, the world's number two producer, declined from 10.6 million barrels per day in 1985 to 9 million barrels in 1991.[6] (See Figure 2.) Industry analysts expect further declines to 7 million barrels a day by the end of the decade.[7]

Of even greater import is the steep decline of the world's top producer, the former Soviet Union (where most of the oil is in Russia). By the time of the country's dissolution in December 1991, Soviet production was down to 10.4 million barrels daily—17 percent below the peak achieved just three years earlier.[8]

The inefficiency of the Soviet economy and recent economic problems are partly responsible, but another factor is the heavily depleted and badly abused oil fields on which the Russian oil industry now relies.[9] In short, the decline will be difficult to reverse. However, the rapid fall in oil use in Russia that is likely once prices are decontrolled will tend to free up more petroleum for export.

It now appears that world oil production is unlikely ever to rise much above the 1979 peak. The large oil fields tapped in the eighties in Mexico, the North Sea, Alaska, and Siberia are no longer expanding, and in some cases are in sharp decline. The only major region with rising production is the Middle East—whose share of the oil market is expected to grow from 27 percent in 1990 to nearly 40 percent by decade's end, according to the International Energy Agency.[10]

The short-term outlook is for continuing excess capacity, and downward pressure on prices is likely. Kuwait and Iraq produced little oil in 1991, and as their production is restored, downward pressure on oil prices is likely. But growth in oil consumption is likely to resume in the mid-nineties, which could eliminate today's spare productive capacity within a few years. And history suggests that the world cannot rely for very long on sustained maximum production in the Middle East.

It is possible that sometime in the late nineties, a new political crisis could lead to another round of oil price increases. There is also hope, however, that growing environmental concerns and accelerated efforts to improve automotive fuel economy and to shift to alternative fuels could reduce global demand for oil quickly enough to avoid another supply crunch.

## WORLD OIL PRODUCTION, 1950–91

| YEAR | PRODUCTION (mill. barrels per day) |
|------|-------------------------------------|
| 1950 | 10.4 |
| 1951 | 11.7 |
| 1952 | 12.4 |
| 1953 | 13.2 |
| 1954 | 13.7 |
| 1955 | 15.4 |
| 1956 | 16.8 |
| 1957 | 17.6 |
| 1958 | 18.1 |
| 1959 | 19.5 |
| 1960 | 21.0 |
| 1961 | 22.4 |
| 1962 | 24.3 |
| 1963 | 26.1 |
| 1964 | 28.2 |
| 1965 | 30.3 |
| 1966 | 32.9 |
| 1967 | 35.4 |
| 1968 | 38.8 |
| 1969 | 41.7 |
| 1970 | 45.8 |
| 1971 | 48.4 |
| 1972 | 51.0 |
| 1973 | 55.8 |
| 1974 | 56.3 |
| 1975 | 53.4 |
| 1976 | 58.1 |
| 1977 | 60.0 |
| 1978 | 60.7 |
| 1979 | 62.7 |
| 1980 | 59.6 |
| 1981 | 55.8 |
| 1982 | 53.1 |
| 1983 | 52.6 |
| 1984 | 54.1 |
| 1985 | 53.4 |
| 1986 | 55.7 |
| 1987 | 55.3 |
| 1988 | 57.7 |
| 1989 | 58.6 |
| 1990 | 59.5 |
| 1991 (est) | 59.0 |

SOURCES: American Petroleum Institute, *Basic Petroleum Data Book* (Washington, D.C.: 1992); 1991 figure is Worldwatch Institute estimate based on British Petroleum, *BP Statistical Review of World Energy* (London: 1992).

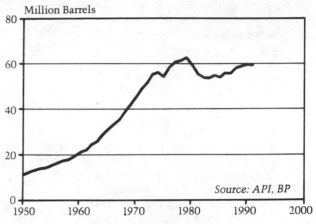

Figure 1: World Oil Production Per Day, 1950–91

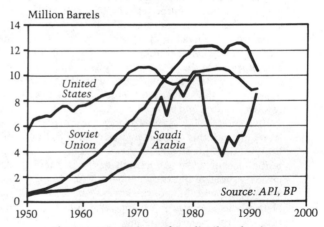

Figure 2: U.S., Soviet, and Saudi Oil Production Per Day, 1950–91

45

# Natural Gas Production Climbs · Christopher Flavin

For the eighth consecutive year, world natural gas production reached a new high in 1991, at 77 trillion cubic feet.[1] (See Figure 1.) The use of this fossil fuel is now growing much faster than either oil or coal, and could well surpass oil as the world's dominant energy source shortly after the year 2000.

Growing demand for natural gas is spurred by its environmental advantages over oil and coal. Natural gas emits only about half as much carbon per unit of energy produced as coal does, and no sulfur, the main cause of acid rain.[2] From Istanbul to Los Angeles, natural gas is being promoted to improve air quality, and is likely to benefit from efforts to slow global warming.

Growth in the use of this fuel has also been propelled by major gas discoveries and by new technologies, such as computer mapping and horizontal drilling, that make it easier to find and extract natural gas in the United States. As a result, the market price for natural gas has recently fallen to the equivalent of $9 per barrel, about half that of oil.[3] Also, unlike oil, reserves are not concentrated in the Middle East. The United States, the world's number two producer, is now estimated to have at least 60 years' worth of gas resources at today's extraction rate.[4]

It was not until an infrastructure to transport, store, and use this gaseous hydrocarbon was first built in the United States in the fifties that its potential became clear. As recently as the late seventies, extensive reserves had been found in just a few areas, and some of the largest—in the Netherlands, for example—appeared to be running out. But experts were missing a key point: most of what was then known about natural gas geology was a by-product of oil exploration. Little effort had been made to identify gas in other areas.[5]

Today, gas exploration is being stepped up, and proven reserves already exceed those of oil, a gap that is likely to widen. During the past two decades, enormous amounts have been discovered in Argentina, Indonesia, Mexico, and central Russia. Each region either is or could become a major exporter of this fuel. Use is also increasing rapidly in Europe, where large North Sea fields provide ever-increasing supplies. Additional gas is imported via pipeline from Russia and North Africa. British coal and nuclear power plans have been abandoned during the past three years in favor of natural gas.[6]

Dozens of other countries have gas reserves that are minor on a global scale, but sufficient to fuel their economies for decades.[7] Yet most developing nations have barely begun to look for this resource. One reason is that large oil companies with capital and technical know-how are less interested in gas, which is not easily sold for hard currency. Moreover, few developing countries have made the investments needed for widespread use of gas.[8]

The world's dominant natural gas producer today is Russia, where despite a decline in oil production, gas is holding roughly steady, reflecting the much larger resource base.[9] (See Figure 2.) Natural gas may be the country's main asset for raising foreign exchange to transform the economy. Large amounts already reach Europe by pipeline, and may soon reach Japan in the same way. A consortium of Japanese companies plans to build a $20-billion undersea pipeline network that would link eastern Siberia with Japan and most of the rest of the Far East, including South Korea and the Philippines.[10]

Estimating the ultimate scale of the worldwide natural gas resource base is still difficult, but available data suggest it is sufficient to at least double the use of gas during the next 20-30 years, and then to sustain that level for several decades. And if gas is used to replace oil and coal, it will help slow global warming.

In the long run, natural gas is likely to be replaced by gaseous hydrogen, a carbon-free fuel that can be produced by solar and other renewable energy sources. Pipelines that now carry natural gas from North Africa and the U.S. Southwest could one day be converted to carry hydrogen. This would allow the evolution of a world energy system that produces virtually no climate-altering carbon dioxide.

## WORLD NATURAL GAS PRODUCTION, 1950–91

| YEAR | PRODUCTION (trill. cu. ft.) |
|------|------------|
| 1950 | 6.7 |
| 1951 | 8.1 |
| 1952 | 8.8 |
| 1953 | 9.5 |
| 1954 | 9.9 |
| 1955 | 10.7 |
| 1956 | 11.6 |
| 1957 | 12.7 |
| 1958 | 13.8 |
| 1959 | 15.4 |
| 1960 | 16.9 |
| 1961 | 18.4 |
| 1962 | 20.1 |
| 1963 | 21.0 |
| 1964 | 22.9 |
| 1965 | 24.5 |
| 1966 | 26.4 |
| 1967 | 28.4 |
| 1968 | 31.4 |
| 1969 | 34.4 |
| 1970 | 38.1 |
| 1971 | 41.2 |
| 1972 | 43.5 |
| 1973 | 46.1 |
| 1974 | 47.2 |
| 1975 | 47.2 |
| 1976 | 49.5 |
| 1977 | 50.1 |
| 1978 | 51.8 |
| 1979 | 57.7 |
| 1980 | 58.6 |
| 1981 | 58.2 |
| 1982 | 55.7 |
| 1983 | 55.3 |
| 1984 | 60.1 |
| 1985 | 62.6 |
| 1986 | 63.8 |
| 1987 | 68.4 |
| 1988 | 71.3 |
| 1989 | 74.4 |
| 1990 | 75.3 |
| 1991 (est) | 77.0 |

SOURCE: American Petroleum Institute, *Basic Petroleum Data Book* (Washington, D.C.: 1992); 1991 figure is Worldwatch Institute estimate based on British Petroleum, *BP Statistical Review of World Energy* (London: 1992).

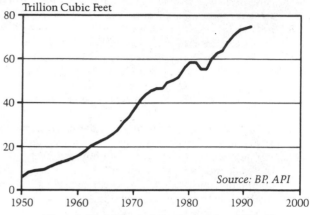

**Figure 1: World Natural Gas Production, 1950–91**

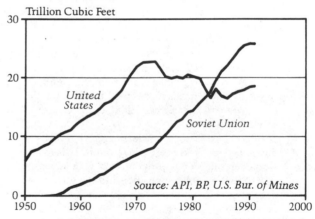

**Figure 2: U.S. and Soviet Natural Gas Production, 1950–91**

# Nuclear Power at Standstill C. Flavin & N. Lenssen

Between 1990 and 1991, total installed nuclear generating capacity declined for the first time since commercial nuclear power began in the fifties. There were 421 nuclear plants in commercial operation in January 1992, fewer than at the peak in 1989. These plants supplied 17 percent of the world's electricity and had a total generating capacity of 326,000 megawatts—only 5 percent above the figure reported 3 years earlier.[1] (See Figure 1.)

Forty-nine nuclear plants are under active construction worldwide, a quarter as many as a decade ago (see Figure 2), with a combined capacity of 39,000 megawatts.[2] Many of these are nearing completion, so in the next few years worldwide nuclear expansion will nearly stop. It now appears that by decade's end the world will have at most 360,000 megawatts of nuclear capacity—only 10 percent above the current figure. This is less than one tenth the figure predicted for the year 2000 by the International Atomic Energy Agency in 1974.[3]

Some 76 reactors, with a total generating capacity of 17,000 megawatts, have already been retired, after an average service life of less than 17 years.[4] As technical problems continue to crop up at many older plants, retirements seem likely to accelerate. Dozens more could be closed in the next few years, nearly cancelling out reactors coming on-line.

In Western Europe, nuclear expansion plans have been stopped everywhere but in France. And even the French program is now in jeopardy due to rising public opposition and the $38-billion debt of the state utility. Only six plants are under construction, and just two have been started since 1987. The United Kingdom has one final plant being completed. Canada and the United States together have just three under construction. No new plants have been ordered in the United States in 14 years, and it has been nearly two decades since a plant was ordered that was not later cancelled.[5]

Japan still has an active nuclear construction program, but there too, public opposition is rising and utility executives are considering alternatives. In the Third World, operating nuclear plants generate 18,000 megawatts—6 percent of the world total.[6] Many are well over budget, behind schedule, and plagued by technical problems. As a consequence, only a handful of orders have been placed in the Third World in the past decade.

Recently, nuclear programs in Eastern Europe and the former Soviet Union have also begun to come unglued. With the arrival of democracy and with some 300,000 people now being treated for radiation sickness, a torrent of public criticism has been unleashed, focusing on the failure of nuclear plants to meet western safety standards.[7] Scores of nuclear plants have been cancelled in Bulgaria, Czechoslovakia, Hungary, Poland, Russia, and the Ukraine.[8] As concern about deteriorating equipment and discipline grow, pressure mounts to close those that remain.

This international trend away from nuclear power is propelled by the two serious accidents at Three Mile Island and Chernobyl, rapid cost escalations, and rising concern about a healthy environment. Many people are worried about the danger of accidents and a continuing failure to develop safe means of disposing of nuclear wastes. Opinion polls in most countries indicate lopsided majorities against the construction of more reactors.[9]

In addition, nuclear costs have risen to the point where nuclear power is no longer competitive with many other energy sources. Not only coal plants, but also new, highly efficient natural gas plants and new technologies such as wind turbines and geothermal energy are less expensive than new nuclear plants.

The old market niche that nuclear power once held is nearly gone. Since 1988, nuclear advocates have tried to use concern about global warming as a reason for reviving the industry, but they have had no impact so far, as reactor orders have continued to dwindle. Nuclear power is an expensive way to offset fossil-fuel-fired power, and several hundred plants would have to be built in order to reduce carbon emissions significantly. Given the current economic and political state of the industry, a major revival seems unlikely.

## WORLD NET INSTALLED ELECTRICAL GENERATING CAPACITY OF NUCLEAR POWER PLANTS, 1950–91

| YEAR | CAPACITY (megawatts) |
|------|---------------------|
| 1950 | 0 |
| 1951 | 0 |
| 1952 | 0 |
| 1953 | 0 |
| 1954 | 5 |
| 1955 | 5 |
| 1956 | 50 |
| 1957 | 100 |
| 1958 | 190 |
| 1959 | 380 |
| 1960 | 830 |
| 1961 | 850 |
| 1962 | 1,800 |
| 1963 | 2,100 |
| 1964 | 3,100 |
| 1965 | 4,800 |
| 1966 | 6,200 |
| 1967 | 8,300 |
| 1968 | 9,200 |
| 1969 | 13,000 |
| 1970 | 16,000 |
| 1971 | 24,000 |
| 1972 | 32,000 |
| 1973 | 45,000 |
| 1974 | 61,000 |
| 1975 | 71,000 |
| 1976 | 85,000 |
| 1977 | 99,000 |
| 1978 | 114,000 |
| 1979 | 121,000 |
| 1980 | 135,000 |
| 1981 | 155,000 |
| 1982 | 170,000 |
| 1983 | 189,000 |
| 1984 | 219,000 |
| 1985 | 250,000 |
| 1986 | 276,000 |
| 1987 | 298,000 |
| 1988 | 311,000 |
| 1989 | 321,000 |
| 1990 | 329,000 |
| 1991 | 326,000 |

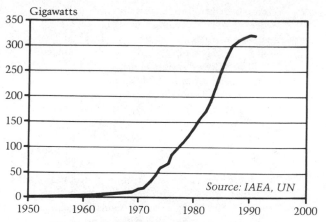

**Figure 1: World Electrical Generating Capacity of Nuclear Power Plants, 1950–91**

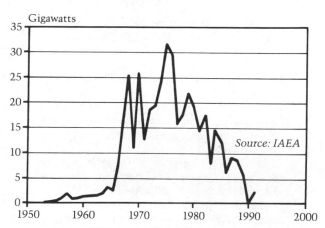

**Figure 2: World Nuclear Reactor Construction Starts, 1950–91**

SOURCES: R. Spiegelberg, Division of Nuclear Power, International Atomic Energy Agency, Vienna, Austria, unpublished printout, March 18, 1992; United Nations, Department of International Economic and Social Affairs, *Energy Statistics Yearbook, 1950–1974* (New York: 1976); Greenpeace International, WISE-Paris, and Worldwatch Institute, *The World Nuclear Industry Status Report: 1992* (London: 1992).

# Wind Power Soars                    Christopher Flavin

Wind power generating capacity increased 17 percent in 1991, reaching a new high of 2,215 megawatts—the equivalent of two large nuclear plants.[1] (See Figure 1.) Wind turbines produced 3.7 billion kilowatt-hours of electricity in 1991—enough for a half-million U.S. homes.[2] While wind power still supplies less than 1 percent of the world's electricity, it is one of the fastest growing sources of energy.

Most wind electricity is delivered by propeller-like turbines, 10 to 30 meters in diameter, that are connected to power generators mounted on tall towers. Modern wind turbines combine sleek aerodynamic blades with high-tech synthetic materials and the latest electronic controls. As a result of such advances, the cost of wind power has fallen from 32¢ per kilowatt-hour in the early eighties to less than 8¢ in 1991.[3] By comparison, new coal-fired plants typically produce power at 5-7¢ per kilowatt-hour.[4]

Most electricity-generating wind turbines have been installed since 1982, when the industry geared up in the wake of new laws that allowed independent power producers in California and Denmark to hook up to utility grids and convey power at a fair price to consumers. As a result, Danish farmers installed wind turbines on their land, and Californian companies, with the help of tax incentives, set up "wind farms" with hundreds of turbines.

Since 1985, companies such as John Hancock Mutual Life Insurance and Aetna Insurance have invested hundreds of millions of dollars in Californian wind farms.[5] Today, the state has more than 15,000 wind turbines concentrated mainly in three areas—Altamont Pass east of San Francisco, the San Gorgonio Pass near Palm Springs, and the Tehachapi Mountains north of Los Angeles. These now produce 1,600 megawatts of power, more than is used by all the homes in San Francisco.[6]

In tiny Denmark, a flat and windy country, wind turbines have been integrated into the agrarian economy during the past decade. They are found throughout the country in ones or twos rather than clusters. Altogether, Denmark has about one fifth as many wind turbines as California, but these provide a full 2 percent of the nation's electricity.[7]

Wind power development slowed briefly in the late eighties, but growing environmental concerns provided a boost during the past two years. European governments have ordered electric utilities to buy wind power at a price that accounts for its environmental advantages—more than double what utilities in California now pay.[8] In addition, new incentive schemes are in place, both nationally and under the auspices of the European Community. As a result, large wind farm projects are being planned in Germany, Italy, the Netherlands, Spain, and the United Kingdom. The European wind industry is expected to triple its installed capacity by 1996, according to a recent survey.[9]

This would easily outpace development in California, where new installations have plateaued as a result of slower growth in power demand and the elimination of tax credits in the mid-eighties. (See Figure 2.) Elsewhere in the United States, large wind farms have been proposed in Minnesota and Iowa, where favorable government policies are now in place.[10] Midwesterners are fond of pointing out that California only ranks eleventh among states in terms of its identified wind power potential.[11]

U.S. government studies show that a quarter of the nation's electricity could be provided by wind farms installed on the windiest 1.5 percent of its land.[12] A windy ridge in Minnesota, less than 640 kilometers from Chicago, could provide one fourth of the power that city now uses. Vast areas of grazing land in the western plains, costing no more than $100 a hectare, could produce $30,000 of power per hectare annually, while still providing grazing for cattle.[13] There are signs that companies are already quietly purchasing the wind rights to thousands of hectares of such land.

Worldwide, wind power could provide many countries with one fifth or more of their electricity.[14] Some of the most promising areas are in North Africa and the trade wind belt around the tropics—including the Caribbean, Central America, and southeast Asia. In Europe, the largest wind farms will likely be placed on offshore platforms in the North and Baltic Seas. Eventually, electricity from the wind may be used to produce hydrogen fuel that can be sent to distant factories and cities.

WORLD WIND ENERGY
GENERATING CAPACITY, 1981–91

| YEAR | CAPACITY (megawatts) |
|------|----------|
| 1981 | 15 |
| 1982 | 80 |
| 1983 | 260 |
| 1984 | 657 |
| 1985 | 971 |
| 1986 | 1,325 |
| 1987 | 1,419 |
| 1988 | 1,385 |
| 1989 | 1,589 |
| 1990 | 1,899 |
| 1991 | 2,215 |

SOURCE: Paul Gipe, American Wind Energy
Association, Tehachapi, Calif., private
communication, April 10, 1992.

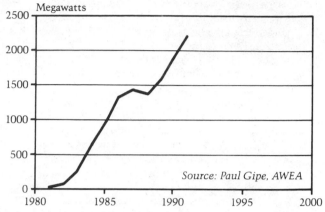

Figure 1: World Wind Energy Generating Capacity, 1981–91

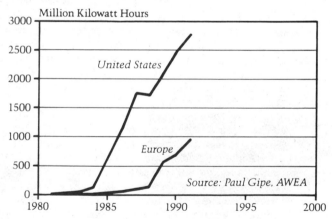

Figure 2: Wind Energy Generation in
United States and Europe, 1981–91

# Solar Cell Production Expanding     Christopher Flavin

Solar electric systems are one of the world's faster growing high-tech industries, having expanded from 2 megawatts in 1975 to 6.5 megawatts in 1980, 23 megawatts in 1985, and 55 megawatts in 1991—an annual growth rate of more than 15 percent, which shows no sign of flattening.[1] (See Figure 1.)

This roughly $500-million-per-year industry is based on photovoltaic solar cells—used to turn sunlight directly into electricity via a photoelectric process. As demand grows and newer production facilities are installed, the cost of solar electricity will fall, and more and more applications will become feasible. This revolutionary technology provides much less than 1 percent of the world's electricity today, but may become a major element of the world energy economy in the future.

Solar cells are electronic devices typically based on silicon—the world's second most abundant element. The standard single crystal silicon cells are now being overtaken by polycrystalline and amorphous silicon, each of which costs much less. They can convert sunlight to electricity with an efficiency ranging from 6 to 12 percent.[2] Meanwhile, newer materials are being developed that could get the efficiency up to 20 percent or more, greatly reducing the area that must be covered with solar cells.[3]

These efficiency improvements, together with the development of lower cost manufacturing processes, have steadily lowered the cost of solar electricity—by a factor of roughly four during the eighties.[4] (See Figure 2.) This has made solar power economically viable for a growing range of uses. But at roughly 30¢ per kilowatt-hour, costs will have to be cut again by a factor of at least three in order to be a competitive source of grid electricity. Many experts believe this will happen within the next decade.[5]

As has happened in so many industries, the Japanese have taken a technology that was developed in the United States and moved to the forefront in commercial applications. Japan is now the leading producer—at 20 megawatts annually—having passed the United States, which produced 17 megawatts in 1991.[6] Europe, led by Germany, came in at 13 megawatts.[7] Japanese and European companies are rapidly boosting their manufacturing capacity. Kyocera of Japan,

for example, plans to spend $23 million to double its plant to a capacity of 12 megawatts per year—equivalent to more than one fifth of the 1991 world market.[8] The German electronics giant Siemens purchased the largest U.S. manufacturer, ARCO Solar, in 1990.[9]

The first solar cells were used to power orbiting satellites, where high cost was not a barrier. Since then, a range of specialized off-grid applications have been developed. Photovoltaics are used at remote lighthouses, fire lookouts, and roadside shelters. In recent years, solar power has been used extensively for telecommunications equipment such as satellite dishes and microwave transmitters. In the mid-eighties, Japanese companies pioneered the use of solar cells in small electronic devices such as hand-held calculators. This market has grown quite large, and the Japanese still dominate it.

The use of solar electricity is now expanding rapidly in the Third World, where it may help meet the needs of more than 1 billion people who do not have power. Many people still rely on kerosene lamps and bulky car batteries—which may have to be hauled long distances for recharging. As an alternative, villagers can purchase a 35- to 50-watt solar package that costs $500-600 and provides enough power to run a television for three hours and four to six light bulbs for three hours each.[10]

More than 1,500 homes have been electrified with photovoltaic cells in the past eight years in the Dominican Republic.[11] Similar programs have been set up in Sri Lanka (where 3,500 homes have been electrified so far) and Zimbabwe.[12] Other countries with major programs of village electrification using solar electricity are India, Indonesia, and French Polynesia.[13]

The next step in the development of solar electricity is to deploy solar cells on rooftops and at desert-based power plants. Several suburban solar homes have already been built in the United States, and large grid-connected systems are being tested as well. By early in the next century, solar electricity may be ubiquitous.

WORLD PHOTOVOLTAIC
SHIPMENTS, 1971–91

| YEAR | SHIPMENTS (megawatts) |
|------|------------------------|
| 1971 | 0.1 |
| 1975 | 1.8 |
| 1976 | 2.0 |
| 1977 | 2.2 |
| 1978 | 2.5 |
| 1979 | 4.0 |
| 1980 | 6.5 |
| 1981 | 7.8 |
| 1982 | 9.1 |
| 1983 | 21.7 |
| 1984 | 25.0 |
| 1985 | 22.8 |
| 1986 | 26.0 |
| 1987 | 29.2 |
| 1988 | 33.8 |
| 1989 | 40.2 |
| 1990 | 46.5 |
| 1991 | 55.3 |

SOURCES: Paul Maycock, *PV
News,* February 1992, February
1985, and February 1982.

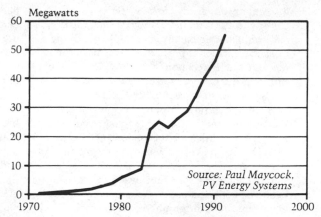

Figure 1: World Photovoltaic Shipments, 1971–91

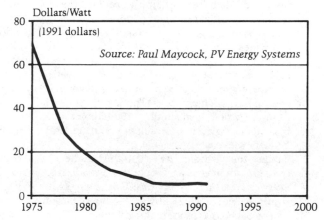

Figure 2: Average Factory Prices for
Photovoltaic Modules, 1975–91

# Energy Efficiency Falls                    Christopher Flavin

The energy efficiency of the world economy fell slightly in 1991, temporarily reversing the trend toward higher efficiency levels. Global energy efficiency, which is measured in terms of the amount of gross economic product produced per unit of primary energy used, was $2,310 per ton of oil equivalent in 1990.[1] (See Figure 1.)

The world is now 17 percent more energy-efficient than at the time of the first major oil crisis in 1973. While global economic activity has increased at an average rate of 3 percent annually since 1980, world energy use has grown at less than 2 percent a year.[2] Improved efficiency levels occurred both because of more efficient technologies—improved automobiles, for example—and because of structural economic changes, such as the decline of heavy industry and the shift to a service-based economy.

Rising energy efficiency reduces the amount of fossil fuels that the world must use, lowering emissions of destructive air pollutants and climate-disrupting greenhouse gases. It is therefore a key measure of the sustainability of the global economy. At the national level, greater energy efficiency tends to improve economic competitiveness by reducing the amount of money that goes to paying energy bills. The United States, for example, would be spending $150 billion a year more on energy if it were still operating at 1973 efficiency levels.[3]

Since the early stages of the Industrial Revolution, growth in economic output has tended to outpace growth in energy use. This is largely the result of technological advances—more-efficient means of cooking food, making steel, running automobiles, and keeping heat inside houses. New compact fluorescent light bulbs are now being installed, for example, that use only a quarter as much power as the incandescent ones they replace.[4] New gas furnaces can reduce the fuel use for heating a home by 30 percent, while additional insulation and high-tech "superwindows" can save another 30 percent.[5] Many such investments have a rate of return of more than 20 percent, and thus a payback period of less than five years.

Industrial nations account for two thirds of world energy use, and have also taken the lead in improving energy efficiency.[6] Since 1973, West Germany's energy efficiency has increased 37 percent, that of the United States has risen 32 percent, and that of Japan 50 percent.[7] (See Figure 2.) Energy efficiency in the United States is less than one third the level in Japan,[8] due to longer travel distances, larger houses, and the failure to modernize industry and buildings.

Centrally planned economies in which energy is cheap tend to be highly inefficient. Russia still has steel plants that would have been considered outmoded in the West in the fifties. And even new apartment buildings have little insulation and no individual heating controls. If Eastern Europe and the Commonwealth of Independent States are to become competitive in today's global economy, they will have to be far more energy-efficient.

Developing countries account for about 25 percent of world primary energy demand, using, in other words, about as much energy as the United States alone.[9] While these countries use a lot less energy than industrial nations do, their buildings, industries, and transportation systems are generally less efficient, often relying on outdated equipment.[10] Given their dependence on imported oil and high levels of air pollution, improved energy efficiency is critical to the futures of most developing nations.

Rising concern about the stability of the global atmosphere has led many countries to accelerate the move to greater energy efficiency, which is by far the cheapest way to keep carbon out of the atmosphere. But new policies are essential: the low energy prices that have prevailed since 1986 have measurably slowed the efficiency trend in many nations. U.S. energy efficiency, for example, is essentially unchanged since 1986.[11]

Home weatherization schemes, appliance efficiency standards, utility conservation programs, higher gasoline taxes, and reduced subsidies to energy production are among the new measures being adopted. The European Community and Japan are also considering new carbon taxes that would discourage the use of coal and oil.[12] If global carbon emissions are to be cut in the years ahead—in the face of a rapidly growing world population—the energy efficiency of the global economy will have to continue rising by at least 2 percent a year.

ENERGY EFFICIENCY OF THE WORLD
ECONOMY, 1950, 1955, AND 1960–91

| YEAR | ENERGY EFFICIENCY[1] |
|------|----------------------|
| 1950 | 1.94 |
| 1955 | 1.94 |
| 1960 | 1.85 |
| 1961 | 1.94 |
| 1962 | 1.92 |
| 1963 | 1.90 |
| 1964 | 1.91 |
| 1965 | 1.92 |
| 1966 | 1.91 |
| 1967 | 1.94 |
| 1968 | 1.91 |
| 1969 | 1.90 |
| 1970 | 1.89 |
| 1971 | 1.94 |
| 1972 | 1.95 |
| 1973 | 1.97 |
| 1974 | 1.99 |
| 1975 | 1.99 |
| 1976 | 1.98 |
| 1977 | 2.00 |
| 1978 | 2.01 |
| 1979 | 2.01 |
| 1980 | 2.10 |
| 1981 | 2.15 |
| 1982 | 2.16 |
| 1983 | 2.20 |
| 1984 | 2.20 |
| 1985 | 2.23 |
| 1986 | 2.23 |
| 1987 | 2.23 |
| 1988 | 2.26 |
| 1989 | 2.29 |
| 1990 | 2.34 |
| 1991 | 2.31 |

[1]Thousand dollars of gross world product per
ton of oil equivalent of world primary energy use.
SOURCES: World Bank, Department of
Socio-Economic Data, Washington, D.C.,
unpublished printout, February 1992; world GNP
data from 1950 and 1955 from Herbert R. Block,
*The Planetary Product in 1980: A Creative Pause?*
(Washington, D.C.: U.S. Department of State,
1981); British Petroleum, *BP Statistical Review of
World Energy* (London: various years).

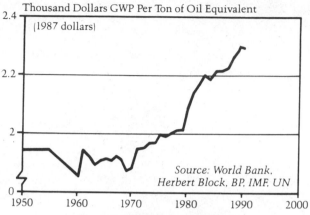

Thousand Dollars GWP Per Ton of Oil Equivalent

(1987 dollars)

Source: World Bank,
Herbert Block, BP, IMF, UN

**Figure 1: World Energy Efficiency,
1950–91**

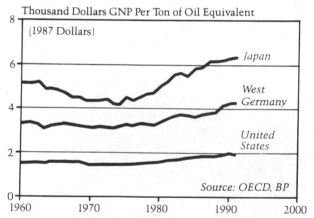

Thousand Dollars GNP Per Ton of Oil Equivalent

(1987 Dollars)

Japan

West
Germany

United
States

Source: OECD, BP

**Figure 2: Energy Efficiency in Japan, United States,
and West Germany, 1960–91**

# Atmospheric
## Trends

# Global Temperature Rises Christopher Flavin

The global average temperature in 1991 was 12.41 degrees Celsius.[1] This makes it the second warmest year in the last century, exceeded only by 1990, according to figures compiled by the U.S. National Aeronautics and Space Administration.[2] (See Figure 1.) If Mount Pinatubo in the Philippines had not erupted in mid-year, creating a cooling effect, 1991 would almost surely have set a new record.

Global average temperatures have increased erratically since recordkeeping began in 1880, with yearly figures influenced by solar cycles, ocean currents, and volcanic eruptions. Nonetheless, temperatures increased fairly steadily from 1880 until 1940, when a minor cooling period began that lasted until the mid-sixties. Since then, global temperatures have soared to record highs. Four of the five warmest years on record have occurred since 1987.[3] Despite Mount Pinatubo's cooling effect, the warming trend is likely to resume by 1995.

Although the increase of 0.5 degrees Celsius over the past two decades may not seem like much, to climatologists it is extremely rapid, far exceeding the normal rate of climate fluctuation. If this trend were to continue for another few decades, it would make the earth warmer than it has been for the past 100,000 years, altering wind and rainfall patterns sufficiently to threaten food production as well as forest and marine ecosystems.[4] Already, many regions appear to be experiencing unusually prolonged droughts and heat waves. The winter of 1991/92, for example, was the warmest ever recorded in the continental United States.[5]

Climatologists have considered a range of possible explanations, but so far one seems most plausible: the rising burden of so-called greenhouse gases that human activities are adding to the atmosphere. These gases—principally carbon dioxide ($CO_2$), chlorofluorocarbons (CFCs), and methane—act like a transparent blanket, letting sunlight through the atmosphere but trapping the resulting heat near the surface. There is a lag in the warming of roughly 20 years, however, since the oceans act as a heat sink, taking a long time to warm up.

Large amounts of carbon only began entering the atmosphere in the fifties, as the global energy economy surged. During the eighties, the amount of carbon released by the burning of fossil fuels climbed to nearly 6 billion tons annually, joined by another 1-2 billion tons from forest burning, mainly in tropical countries.[6] This led to a rapid rise in the concentration of $CO_2$ in the atmosphere—from 316 parts per million when continuous recordkeeping began in 1959 to 355 parts per million in 1991, an increase of 12 percent.[7] (See Figure 2.) Meanwhile, methane concentrations have been rising at 1 percent a year and CFCs at 5 percent annually.[8]

The amount of warming since 1950 is roughly consistent with the additional greenhouse gases added to the atmosphere during the period. In fact, new data suggest that previously unexplained anomalies may have relatively straightforward explanations. For example, it seems that nighttime temperatures are rising faster than daytime ones and that southern latitude temperatures are increasing more rapidly than in the north, perhaps because sulfates and other aerosols produced by industrial pollution are reducing the amount of sunlight reaching northern latitudes. Since air pollution levels are beginning to fall in many regions as a result of emission controls, these aerosols are unlikely to offset future warming.[9]

For most scientists, the record so far amounts to circumstantial evidence rather than definitive proof of human-induced global warming. Just as it typically takes six months after a recession begins before economists have enough data to officially recognize it, so are scientists now trying to confirm a greenhouse warming that may already be under way.

Climate scientists use complex global circulation models to predict how much the climate might change as a result of the greenhouse gases now being added. The 1992 scientific report by the U.N.-sponsored Intergovernmental Panel on Climate Change (IPCC), which includes over 100 leading scientists, projects that global temperatures will rise by between 1.5 and 4.5 degrees Celsius by 2050 as a result of the effective doubling of $CO_2$ concentrations. The IPCC concluded that such a rapid warming could disrupt water and food supplies for millions of people, and threaten the survival of many plant and animal species.[10]

GLOBAL AVERAGE TEMPERATURE, 1950–91

| YEAR | DEGREES CELSIUS |
|------|-----------------|
| 1950 | 11.87 |
| 1951 | 11.99 |
| 1952 | 12.05 |
| 1953 | 12.15 |
| 1954 | 11.94 |
| 1955 | 11.95 |
| 1956 | 11.84 |
| 1957 | 12.11 |
| 1958 | 12.11 |
| 1959 | 12.06 |
| 1960 | 12.01 |
| 1961 | 12.09 |
| 1962 | 12.03 |
| 1963 | 12.03 |
| 1964 | 11.75 |
| 1965 | 11.85 |
| 1966 | 11.92 |
| 1967 | 11.99 |
| 1968 | 11.89 |
| 1969 | 12.04 |
| 1970 | 12.05 |
| 1971 | 11.90 |
| 1972 | 11.95 |
| 1973 | 12.20 |
| 1974 | 11.94 |
| 1975 | 11.96 |
| 1976 | 11.79 |
| 1977 | 12.17 |
| 1978 | 12.10 |
| 1979 | 12.15 |
| 1980 | 12.29 |
| 1981 | 12.40 |
| 1982 | 12.08 |
| 1983 | 12.30 |
| 1984 | 12.12 |
| 1985 | 12.12 |
| 1986 | 12.17 |
| 1987 | 12.33 |
| 1988 | 12.35 |
| 1989 | 12.25 |
| 1990 | 12.47 |
| 1991 | 12.41 |

SOURCES: J. Hansen and S. Lebedeff, "Global Surface Air Temperatures: Update through 1987," *Geophysical Research Letters,* Vol. 15, No. 4, 1988; Helene Wilson, NASA Goddard Institute for Space Studies, New York, private communication, March 23, 1992.

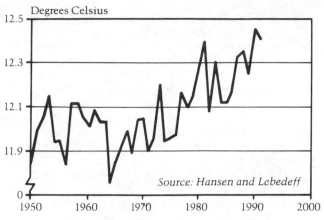

Figure 1: Global Average Temperature, 1950–91

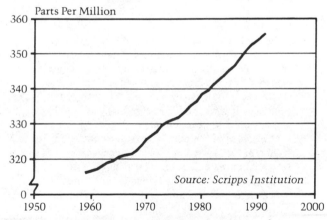

Figure 2: Atmospheric Concentrations of
Carbon Dioxide, 1959-91

# Carbon Emissions Steady
## Christopher Flavin

Global emissions of carbon from fossil fuel burning, the most important contributor to global warming, rose only slightly in 1990 and 1991.[1] Although this levelling off is welcome, it does not represent the turnaround in global energy trends needed to stabilize the climate. The new figures do suggest, however, that cutting carbon emissions is easier than most governments seem to recognize.

Nearly 6 billion tons of carbon are released into the atmosphere through fossil fuel burning each year (see Figure 1), and another 1-2 billion tons from deforestation.[2] Total emissions of carbon, the chief product of fossil fuel combustion, now occur at two to three times the rate the world's oceans and forests can absorb them—leading to steady increases in atmospheric concentrations of the heat-trapping gas carbon dioxide.[3]

Global emissions of carbon have risen throughout most of the twentieth century, culminating in a greater than threefold increase since 1950. During this 40 years, however, emission growth rates have slowed—from 4.6 percent annually in the fifties and sixties to 2.5 percent in the seventies and 1.3 percent in the eighties.[4] The main reasons are higher oil prices, which encouraged greater energy efficiency, new energy technologies, and slowed economic expansion in developing countries—itself provoked in part by the cost of oil and spiralling external debt.

One cause of the slower growth in emissions in 1990 and 1991 was the economic recession in North America and other industrial regions. As a result, carbon emissions from advanced industrial nations, which contribute nearly half the world total, have held about steady for the past two years.[5]

The second reason is that energy use and carbon emissions have begun to fall rapidly in the former Soviet bloc. (See Figure 2.) In Eastern Europe, emissions in 1991 were already 22 percent lower than in 1987, and further declines are likely. In the former Soviet republics, the decline is still picking up speed—but emissions had already fallen 10 percent between 1988 and 1991.[6] Much of the uncompetitive industrial base of this region is gradually being shut down.

As the members of the Commonwealth of Independent States proceed with economic restructuring, including the decontrol of still heavily subsidized energy prices, further declines in carbon emissions are inevitable. Economic recovery will have to rely on far more efficient energy conversion and end-use technologies, including new factories and renovated buildings. Many existing uses of coal will likely be replaced by combined-cycle gas turbines—yielding a 60-percent reduction in carbon emissions per kilowatt-hour.[7] Taken together, these trends suggest a greater than 30 percent decline in C.I.S. and East European emissions by the mid-nineties. Although emissions will eventually rebound, they may never regain the 1987 peak.

These trends have worldwide significance since Eastern Europe had some of the highest per capita carbon emission, and the former Soviet Union is the world's number two emitter—just behind the United States.[8] A 30-percent cut in C.I.S. emissions translates into a 5-percent cut globally. As a result, global emissions may stay near 1991 levels through the mid-nineties.

Although developing countries have contributed only minimally to global warming so far, they are expected to produce a rising share of emissions during the next several decades. The Third World contains three quarters of the world's population, but carbon emissions per capita are between one fiftieth and one fifth the level in industrial nations.[9] Unless these countries gain access to more energy-efficient technologies, their increased emissions could offset the reductions achieved elsewhere.

Atmospheric concentrations of carbon dioxide will not stabilize until carbon emissions return at least to the 1950 level of less than 2 billion tons annually. This implies a restructuring of the global energy economy, greatly improving energy efficiency, and shifting from reliance on oil and coal to renewable energy sources. As a first step, some 27 industrial countries have already set goals to limit carbon emissions, including Germany, which plans a 25-percent reduction by 2005.[10] The global climate treaty signed at the Earth Summit in Rio may provide further impetus.

## WORLD CARBON EMISSIONS FROM BURNING FOSSIL FUELS, 1950–91

| YEAR | EMISSIONS (mill. met. tons) |
|---|---|
| 1950 | 1,620 |
| 1951 | 1,755 |
| 1952 | 1,781 |
| 1953 | 1,824 |
| 1954 | 1,844 |
| 1955 | 2,020 |
| 1956 | 2,153 |
| 1957 | 2,244 |
| 1958 | 2,302 |
| 1959 | 2,431 |
| 1960 | 2,543 |
| 1961 | 2,557 |
| 1962 | 2,659 |
| 1963 | 2,804 |
| 1964 | 2,959 |
| 1965 | 3,095 |
| 1966 | 3,251 |
| 1967 | 3,355 |
| 1968 | 3,526 |
| 1969 | 3,735 |
| 1970 | 4,013 |
| 1971 | 4,158 |
| 1972 | 4,320 |
| 1973 | 4,553 |
| 1974 | 4,560 |
| 1975 | 4,534 |
| 1976 | 4,792 |
| 1977 | 4,926 |
| 1978 | 4,966 |
| 1979 | 5,247 |
| 1980 | 5,144 |
| 1981 | 5,008 |
| 1982 | 4,973 |
| 1983 | 4,960 |
| 1984 | 5,115 |
| 1985 | 5,238 |
| 1986 | 5,415 |
| 1987 | 5,519 |
| 1988 | 5,747 |
| 1989 | 5,815 |
| 1990 | 5,830 |
| 1991 (est) | 5,854 |

SOURCES: Thomas A. Boden et al., *Trends '91: A Compendium of Data on Global Change* (Oak Ridge, Tenn.: Oak Ridge National Laboratory, 1991); British Petroleum, *BP Statistical Review of World Energy* (London: 1992).

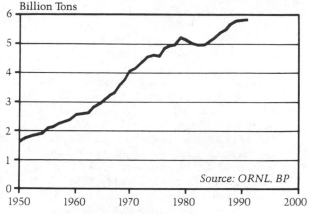

**Figure 1: World Carbon Emissions from Fossil Fuel Burning, 1950–91**

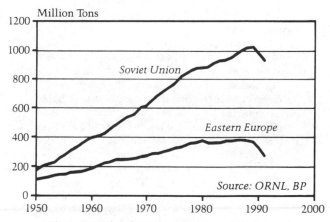

**Figure 2: Carbon Emissions from Fossil Fuel Burning in Soviet Union and Eastern Europe, 1950–91**

# CFC Production Falling Fast
Lester R. Brown

From 1990 to 1991, production of chlorofluoro-carbons (CFCs), the family of chemicals depleting the stratospheric ozone layer, dropped 16 percent. (See Figures 1 and 2.) Since the peak year in 1988, it has fallen 46 percent—an impressive achievement, and an example of how the international community can act in the common interest.[1]

Although the U.S. Congress passed a law in 1978 banning the use of CFCs as propellants in aerosol cans, effective international action was not taken until the Montreal Protocol of 1987. Signed by 36 countries, including all the major CFC producers, it called for a 20-percent cut in production by 1993, and an additional 30-percent cut by 1998. This was followed by a 1990 meeting in London where 92 countries agreed to phase out CFC production by 2000.[2]

Late in 1991, an international scientific assessment concluded that the ozone layer in temperate latitudes was being depleted in the summer as well as in winter and spring.[3] At that time the weight of evidence suggested that this ozone depletion was caused by the presence of human-made chlorine and bromine. In early 1992, new findings provided further support for this conclusion.[4] Facing the prospect of increases in ultraviolet radiation in the northern tier of industrial countries, many national governments decided to accelerate the phaseout of CFC production.

The United States announced it would advance its ban on CFC production from the end of 1999 to the end of 1995. Shortly thereafter, the 12 environment ministers of the European Community endorsed a phaseout of all CFC use by the end of December 1995. Some governments moved even faster: Denmark is banning CFC use by the end of 1994, while Germany is contemplating doing so by the end of 1993.[5]

At the corporate level, some companies are moving faster than others but many are moving faster than national governments. In 1991, for instance, E.I. Du Pont de Nemours and Company committed to phasing out CFC production before the U.S. deadline.[6] In Canada, Northern Telecom, an international electronics company, announced in early 1992 that it had stopped using CFCs as solvents in its 42 facilities worldwide.[7]

The next step in limiting chlorine concentrations in the atmosphere is to recycle the chemicals already in existing refrigerators and air conditioners. In the United Kingdom, many refrigerator retailers will take back an old model and recover the refrigerant when a customer buys a new one.[8] In Germany, the Waste Management and Recycling Company in Seigburg near Bonn recovers CFCs from both the foam and the refrigerating units in the 6,000 refrigerators it recycles each month.[9]

The various government and industry initiatives are in response to scientific evidence that CFCs break down in the upper atmosphere, creating free-chlorine atoms that interact with ozone, producing chlorine monoxide and oxygen and slowly depleting the ozone supply.[10] The rule of thumb is that each 1-percent loss in stratospheric ozone leads to a 1- to 2-percent increase in the amount of ultraviolet radiation reaching the earth's surface.[11]

Public concern about this problem initially focused on how increased ultraviolet radiation would affect human health. It means higher levels of skin cancer, including the often-fatal malignant melanoma, increased eye damage, and a suppression of the human immune system.[12] Epidemiologists estimate that each 1-percent loss of stratospheric ozone leads to a rise in incidence of skin cancer of 3 percent or more.[13]

But agriculture and natural ecosystems are also vulnerable. Ongoing research in Australia and in the Philippines indicates that increased ultraviolet radiation damages basic food crops, such as wheat and rice. Among other things, it impedes the process of photosynthesis and reduces nutrient uptake, thereby stunting growth.[14] Scientists are finding that each 1-percent increase in ultraviolet radiation leads to a 1-percent decline in the yield of some varieties of soybeans, one of the more radiation-sensitive crops.[15]

Although the international response to the use of these destructive chemicals is heartening, it can take up to 15 years for CFCs to reach the upper atmosphere when they are released by human activities. Once there, they can remain active for many decades.[16] Thus even with a complete phaseout of CFC production during the nineties, the risk of stratospheric ozone depletion will continue for at least several decades.

ESTIMATED GLOBAL CFC PRODUCTION, 1950–91

| YEAR | TOTAL | PROPELLANT |
|------|-------|------------|
| | (thousand met. tons) | |
| 1950 | 42 | — |
| 1951 | 75 | — |
| 1952 | 52 | — |
| 1953 | 65 | — |
| 1954 | 71 | — |
| 1955 | 86 | — |
| 1956 | 103 | — |
| 1957 | 110 | — |
| 1958 | 105 | — |
| 1959 | 125 | — |
| 1960 | 150 | 121 |
| 1961 | 170 | 137 |
| 1962 | 210 | 171 |
| 1963 | 250 | 195 |
| 1964 | 290 | 228 |
| 1965 | 330 | 255 |
| 1966 | 390 | 296 |
| 1967 | 440 | 333 |
| 1968 | 510 | 379 |
| 1969 | 580 | 421 |
| 1970 | 640 | 467 |
| 1971 | 690 | 492 |
| 1972 | 790 | 546 |
| 1973 | 900 | 619 |
| 1974 | 970 | 670 |
| 1975 | 860 | 480 |
| 1976 | 920 | 485 |
| 1977 | 880 | 406 |
| 1978 | 880 | 366 |
| 1979 | 850 | 317 |
| 1980 | 880 | 310 |
| 1981 | 890 | 293 |
| 1982 | 870 | 284 |
| 1983 | 950 | 293 |
| 1984 | 1,050 | 304 |
| 1985 | 1,090 | 310 |
| 1986 | 1,130 | 316 |
| 1987 | 1,250 | 321 |
| 1988 | 1,260 | 275 |
| 1989 | 1,150 | 198 |
| 1990 | 810 | 169 |
| 1991 | 680 | 125 |

SOURCE: Data for 1950–59 are Worldwatch Institute estimates based on data from Chemical Manufacturers Association; data for 1960–91 from E.I. Du Pont de Nemours, Wilmington, Del., private communication, April 15, 1992.

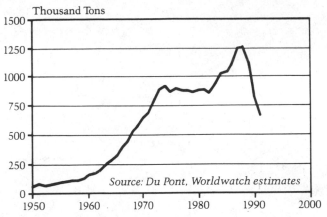

Figure 1: World Production of Chlorofluorocarbons, 1950–91

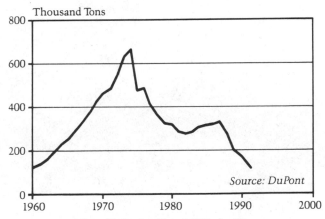

Figure 2: Production of CFCs for Use as Aerosol Propellants, 1960–91

# Economic Trends

In 1991, the world output of goods and services fell slightly, to $18.7 trillion, a loss of 0.3 percent from 1990. (See Figure 1.) The first drop since World War II, it led to an even larger decline in per capita gross world product because population continued to grow.[1] (See Figure 2.)

The recession in the United States accounted for part of the global slowdown, as U.S. output fell by 0.7 percent in 1991.[2] In Germany and Japan, both economic pacesetters, central banks kept interest rates high in order to discourage inflation, thus slowing growth. The dismantling of the Soviet Union and efforts throughout Eastern Europe to shift to market economies disrupted production, dropping economic output there by a remarkable 16.9 percent in 1991.[3]

Many developing countries registered economic growth even though they continue to struggle with indebtedness and other problems of development. The average economic production of all developing countries increased by 3.3 percent in 1991, continuing several years of growth.[4] But this average conceals diverse performances. Growth was highest for Asian countries, at 5.8 percent. For Latin America, it was 2.8 percent. And Africa had 1.4 percent economic growth, falling slightly short of population increase.[5]

From the mid-forties until the 1973 oil shock, the world economy grew rapidly, with the annual increase staying around 5 percent over many years. Between 1950 and 1973, the worldwide output of goods and services tripled, from $3.8 trillion to $11.7 trillion.[6] Since 1973, however, growth of the economy has slowed while that of population has continued at 1.7 percent per year. Hence, production per person has risen more slowly, and during several years it declined. While per capita output doubled from $1,500 in 1950 to nearly $3,000 in 1973, it had only increased to $3,500 by 1991.[7]

In the regions with the most rapid population growth, production per capita has actually fallen. With birth rates high among the poor, the cycles of underdevelopment and population growth have acted as a drag on productive capacities.

After steady per capita growth in output during the seventies, Africa south of the Sahara watched its gross national product (GNP) per person decline sharply in the early and mid-eighties. (See Figure 3.) From a high of $430 in 1981, the product per person dropped to $340 at the end of the decade.[8]

In Latin America, GNP per capita fell rapidly during the first five years of the eighties, the time of the onset of the debt crisis, after growing rapidly between 1973 and 1980. Even after recovering somewhat later in the decade, per capita GNP was still less than $2,000 per person, down nearly 7 percent from $2,140 in 1981.[9]

By contrast, through 1989, economic output per person in the 23 richest countries grew in all but two years—1982 and 1983—and usually grew substantially. Between 1973 and 1991, the average rate of growth of GNP among those countries was 2.5 percent each year.[10]

It is widely acknowledged that economic trends as measured by GNP do not always signify human progress. They do not include unpaid labor, such as household work, even though it can have considerable value; they mask large differences in regional purchasing power, and therefore misrepresent quality of life; they do not account for differences among income groups; and they do not include environmental losses, among other shortcomings.

If national economic accounting systems were to incorporate the depletion of natural capital and the external costs of air pollution, global warming, or other negative effects of economic activity in their calculations, world economic growth would be much less than is now reported. If such things as forest losses from acid rain, topsoil losses from overplowing, or species losses from forest clearing were included, economic accounts would not look nearly as good. And if the health care costs associated with air pollution or the costs of cleaning up toxic waste sites were included, the list of countries with falling GNP per capita during the eighties would undoubtedly be much longer than the 43 reported by the World Bank.[11]

## GROSS WORLD PRODUCT, 1950–91

| YEAR | TOTAL (trillion 1987 dollars) | PER CAPITA (1987 dollars) |
|------|------|------|
| 1950 | 3.8 | 1,501 |
| 1955 | 4.9 | 1,766 |
| 1960 | 6.1 | 2,018 |
| 1961 | 6.4 | 2,065 |
| 1962 | 6.7 | 2,129 |
| 1963 | 7.0 | 2,191 |
| 1964 | 7.5 | 2,290 |
| 1965 | 7.9 | 2,361 |
| 1966 | 8.3 | 2,433 |
| 1967 | 8.6 | 2,475 |
| 1968 | 9.1 | 2,566 |
| 1969 | 9.7 | 2,666 |
| 1970 | 10.1 | 2,732 |
| 1971 | 10.5 | 2,772 |
| 1972 | 11.0 | 2,857 |
| 1973 | 11.7 | 2,974 |
| 1974 | 11.8 | 2,961 |
| 1975 | 11.9 | 2,916 |
| 1976 | 12.5 | 3,006 |
| 1977 | 13.0 | 3,076 |
| 1978 | 13.5 | 3,137 |
| 1979 | 14.0 | 3,193 |
| 1980 | 14.1 | 3,176 |
| 1981 | 14.3 | 3,170 |
| 1982 | 14.4 | 3,123 |
| 1983 | 14.8 | 3,152 |
| 1984 | 15.4 | 3,233 |
| 1985 | 16.0 | 3,307 |
| 1986 | 16.4 | 3,326 |
| 1987 | 17.0 | 3,381 |
| 1988 | 17.8 | 3,478 |
| 1989 | 18.4 | 3,532 |
| 1990 | 18.8 | 3,548 |
| 1991 | 18.7 | 3,477 |

SOURCES: World Bank Department of Socio-Economic Data and IMF; gross world product data for 1950 and 1955 from Herbert R. Block, *The Planetary Product in 1980: A Creative Pause?* (Washington, D.C.: U.S. Department of State, 1981).

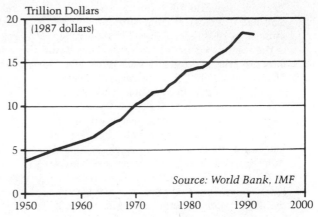

**Figure 1: Gross World Product, 1950–91**

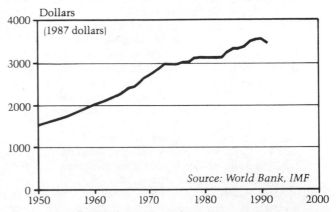

**Figure 2: Gross World Product Per Person, 1950–91**

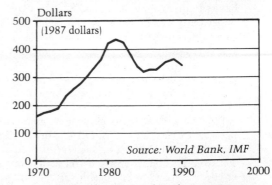

**Figure 3: Gross National Product Per Person for Sub-Saharan Africa, 1970–90**

* Excluding Nigeria.

# Third World Debt Persists                    Hal Kane

In 1991, the world's developing countries had an external debt of $1.35 trillion, essentially the same as in 1990.[1] (See Figure 1.) This levelling off in the last few years follows a period of extraordinary growth. Between 1980 and 1987, debt doubled from $639 billion to nearly $1.3 trillion, reaching a level so burdensome that it stifled development in much of the Third World.[2]

In a sense, the debt crisis had its origins in 1973 with the first oil shock, and it gained momentum with the second oil shock, in 1979. Oil-exporting countries found themselves with suddenly swelling bankrolls, and western banks were eager to put that money into large investments. Developing countries, which suffered from the increased cost of oil and needed financing to stimulate development, received the "petro-dollars" with open arms.

In the early eighties several developments converged to create the debt crisis. Interest rates soared as the United States borrowed heavily in world capital markets to finance its budget deficit. The combination of high interest rates, a global recession in the early eighties, and weak commodity prices throughout the decade created an international financial crisis. Most important, many of the earlier loans had been wasted through inefficiency and corruption, and hence failed to generate income that otherwise could have gone toward their repayment.

After a point, the crisis mentality began to feed on itself. Wealthy investors in developing countries transferred increasing amounts of capital to banks in the United States and Europe. Economic uncertainty had fueled a "capital flight" that further undermined Third World economies. The result was a proliferation of debt. By 1987, the external debt in some of the poorest countries was larger than the annual gross national product. In the case of Zambia, the debt was three times as large.[3]

Extreme indebtedness has made it all but impossible for developing countries to invest adequately in their futures through forest protection, soil conservation, energy-efficient technologies, or education and public health. On the contrary, crushing debts have compelled them to sell off natural resources, often their only source of foreign currency. Like a consumer forced to hock the family heirlooms to pay credit card bills, developing countries are plundering forests, decimating fisheries, and depleting water supplies—regardless of the long-term consequences.[4]

In terms of ability to pay off debt, sub-Saharan Africa was in the weakest position. In 1989 the region's external debt was almost four times as large as its annual earnings from exports. Latin America was not far behind, with an external debt of almost three times its yearly export earnings.[5]

By the mid-eighties, new private investments into the Third World had virtually dried up. This combined with the heavy servicing of debt to create a situation from 1984 through 1988 where the net transfer of capital was from developing countries to industrial ones. (See Figure 2.) This total negative transfer reached $12 billion in 1987 (at which point poor countries were paying rich ones $50 billion more in the interest and principal on old loans than they received in new loans).[6]

Soon thereafter, however, the weight of the negative transfers lessened, and the following year a positive net exchange from industrial to developing countries was restored, due in part to initiatives by governments and international organizations to reschedule debt payments.

In a few cases, northern governments have gone farther and forgiven part of the debt. In late 1987, Canada decided to eliminate $561 million of outstanding loans to sub-Saharan governments. Likewise, Britain cancelled $1.7 billion worth of old aid loans to the poorest countries. In 1989, the United States announced it would do the same for $735 million owed to it by 12 sub-Saharan countries. And West Germany forgave $3.8 billion of debt owed by 28 African countries.[7] More recently, some politicians have called for additional debt forgiveness,[8] but they have been held up by a lack of consensus among the Group of Seven nations.

While the debt "crisis" has now eased, at least as far as the large private banks are concerned, debt servicing continues to be a major drag on Third World economies.

As long as indebtedness continues at levels as high as over 40 percent of the collective gross national product of the Third World,[9] it will continue to deny three quarters of the world's population the resources required for development.

## EXTERNAL DEBT OF ALL DEVELOPING COUNTRIES, 1980–91

| YEAR | DEBT (bill. dollars) |
|------|------|
| 1980 | 639 |
| 1981 | 751 |
| 1982 | 846 |
| 1983 | 912 |
| 1984 | 943 |
| 1985 | 1,046 |
| 1986 | 1,147 |
| 1987 | 1,290 |
| 1988 | 1,282 |
| 1989 | 1,306 |
| 1990 | 1,355 |
| 1991 | 1,351 |

## TOTAL NET TRANSFERS OF CAPITAL FROM INDUSTRIAL TO DEVELOPING COUNTRIES, 1980–91

| YEAR | NET TRANSFER (bill. dollars) |
|------|------|
| 1980 | 37 |
| 1981 | 46 |
| 1982 | 29 |
| 1983 | 14 |
| 1984 | 0 |
| 1985 | − 5 |
| 1986 | − 7 |
| 1987 | − 12 |
| 1988 | − 6 |
| 1989 | 4 |
| 1990 | 16 |
| 1991 | 12 |

SOURCE: World Bank, *World Debt Tables 1991–92* (Washington, D.C.: 1992).

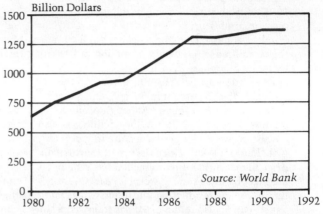

**Figure 1: External Debt of Developing Countries, 1980–91**

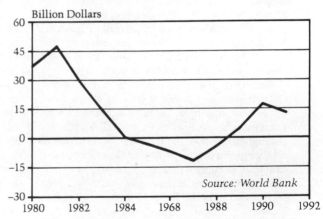

**Figure 2: Net Movement of Public and Private Capital from Industrial to Developing Countries, 1980–91**

# Automobile Production Drops                        Ed Ayres

World auto production fell by 2.9 percent in 1991, with recession taking its toll in all the major manufacturing regions. (See Figure 1.) The number of passenger cars assembled fell by more than a million, from nearly 36 million in 1990 to less than 35 million.[1]

Production dropped by 10.5 percent in the United States, 5 percent in Europe, and slightly under 2 percent in Japan.[2] Although economic slumps were a major factor, the decline was also consistent with a longer-term flattening of the global auto market. Since the eve of the 1979 oil price hike, world auto production has grown, on average, by less than 1 percent a year. Overall motor vehicle production (including trucks and vans), which also fell in 1991, has followed a similar long-term pattern.

In a few countries, primarily in the developing world, production increased in 1991. South Korea topped the 1-million mark for the first time, up 23 percent from 1990.[3] Production increased by 20 percent in Mexico, and 5 percent in Spain and Brazil.[4] China had the largest percentage increase, but from a very small base—from 24,000 cars in 1990 to about 32,000 in 1991.[5]

These regional increases in production occurred primarily as a result of growing demand in developing countries. Globally, however, they were more than offset by sharp declines in sales throughout most of the industrial world. Without a surge in purchases by former East Germans, for example, European production would have been much lower. Sales of passenger cars were down by 21 percent in the United Kingdom, 18 percent in Sweden, 14 percent in Norway, 12 percent in France, and 10 percent in Spain.[6]

In the United States, the sharp decline in production reflected not only the effects of severe recession (sales of cars and light trucks fell by 11.2 percent), but also a continuing restructuring of the industry.[7] The 1991 total of 5.4 million cars produced was 44 percent below the peak level of 1973. Indeed, fewer cars were produced in the United States in 1991 than 40 years ago. The U.S. share of world production has fallen from its high of 81 percent in 1950 to just 16 percent in 1991.[8]

The long-term trends suggest that the world auto market may have entered an era of much slower growth. In the boom years after the end of World War II, worldwide car production grew 6 percent a year for more than two decades.[9] Since the 1974-75 recession, it has been erratic. Motor vehicle manufacturers had hoped that the developing world would follow the U.S. pattern of high auto ownership, but this is not happening.

While the growth in auto ownership has slowed, the total number of cars on the road continues to climb—and was projected to pass 450 million in 1992.[10] (See Figure 2.) Except in a few nations with rising incomes, growth in the world's auto fleet over the last decade has been more a reflection of population growth than of increasing rates of car ownership, however. In most countries, both industrial and developing, the average number of people per car has declined only slightly—from about 13.5 to 12—since 1982. (See Figure 3.) In the United States, it has remained at about 2 people per car since the early seventies.[11]

It may not be known for several years how much this appearance of a saturation in the market for autos is due to temporary economic conditions. The nineties may see significant increases in car ownership in the former Soviet Union, Eastern Europe, East Asia, and Latin America. But it is noteworthy that the flattening of the growth curve is a two-tiered phenomenon, with most of the poorer countries showing few signs of being able to jump to the track of high car ownership.

The most likely explanation is that only a small portion of the world's people have the income needed to buy cars, and as long as personal income remains low in much of the developing world, the auto market will have little room to grow. Further constraints may be imposed by such factors as the diminishing availability of land for automotive infrastructure, the capital cost of highway construction and maintenance, and the congestion and air pollution in cities throughout the world.

WORLD AUTOMOBILE PRODUCTION,
1950–91

| YEAR | PRODUCTION (million) |
|------|------------|
| 1950 | 8 |
| 1951 | 7 |
| 1952 | 6 |
| 1953 | 8 |
| 1954 | 8 |
| 1955 | 11 |
| 1956 | 9 |
| 1957 | 10 |
| 1958 | 9 |
| 1959 | 11 |
| 1960 | 13 |
| 1961 | 11 |
| 1962 | 14 |
| 1963 | 16 |
| 1964 | 17 |
| 1965 | 19 |
| 1966 | 19 |
| 1967 | 19 |
| 1968 | 22 |
| 1969 | 23 |
| 1970 | 22 |
| 1971 | 26 |
| 1972 | 28 |
| 1973 | 30 |
| 1974 | 26 |
| 1975 | 25 |
| 1976 | 29 |
| 1977 | 30 |
| 1978 | 31 |
| 1979 | 31 |
| 1980 | 29 |
| 1981 | 28 |
| 1982 | 27 |
| 1983 | 30 |
| 1984 | 30 |
| 1985 | 32 |
| 1986 | 33 |
| 1987 | 33 |
| 1988 | 34 |
| 1989 | 36 |
| 1990 | 36 |
| 1991 | 35 |

SOURCES: Motor Vehicle Manufacturers
Association and Worldwatch Institute
estimates.

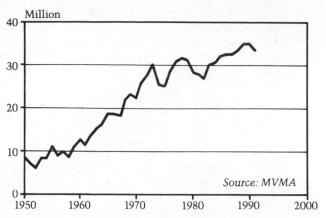

**Figure 1: World Automobile Production, 1950–91**

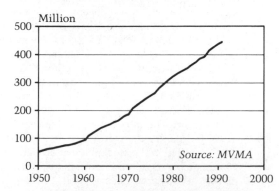

**Figure 2: World Automobile Fleet, 1950–91**

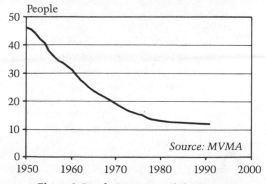

**Figure 3: People Per Automobile, 1950–91**

# Bicycle Production Outpaces Autos     Marcia D. Lowe

World output of bicycles totalled an estimated 95 million in 1990, more than two and a half times the number of automobiles produced.[1] (See Figure 1.) Since 1960, the first year for which worldwide data are available, the number of bicycles produced has quintupled.[2] Today the world bicycle fleet totals some 850 million, nearly double the roughly 450 million cars on the road.[3] With the enormous surge in bike ownership during the last 15 years, the bicycle has replaced the car as the leading vehicle for personal transportation.

After remaining remarkably stable from 1960 to 1969, ranging from 20-25 million per year, bike production doubled to 52 million in 1973 as environmental and recreational interests in the industrial countries turned many to bicycles. Surging oil prices helped sustain production during the mid-seventies, and then economic reforms in China unleashed an enormous pent-up demand for mobility among the one fifth of humanity residing there. For the next decade, growth in world bicycle-building closely tracked that in China, which went from under 10 million to more than 40 million between 1976 and 1987.[4] (See Figure 2.)

The record output of 44 million bikes in China in 1988—pushing the world figure past 105 million—resulted in the stockpiling of an estimated 13 million bicycles in the saturated domestic market.[5] Production fell sharply in 1989 and again in 1990, to some 32 million bicycles. But in 1990, India (the second largest producer) and Italy (the eighth) each increased their output substantially, partly offsetting the cutback in China.[6]

With growth in the industry since 1980 concentrated in Asia, the region's share of output is expanding. It now accounts for 64 percent of the world total—up from 43 percent in 1980. North America's and Western Europe's shares each declined by more than half in the same period; the Soviet and East European share dropped from 14 to 10 percent.[7]

Among industrial countries, the United States currently produces 5.6 million bikes.[8] (See Figure 3.) Japan, the largest industrial-world producer, has an output of just under 8 million.[9] In contrast to the United States, where most bicycles are used mainly by children or recreational riders, bikes in Japan are widely used for commuting.

Among Third World producers, Taiwan is making the greatest gains in exports to industrial-country markets. In 1990, a third of its exports went to Europe and nearly half to North America.[10] China, finding it difficult to compete with the quality of Taiwanese bicycles, recently turned its export efforts to West Africa and Latin America.[11] The Indian government has also promoted bicycle exports since the eighties.[12]

Although at least 25 developing countries besides China, India, and Taiwan have domestic bicycle industries, the only other world-scale producer is Brazil. In 1990, Brazil turned out 2 million bicycles, 10 times the number it had produced three decades earlier.[13] The greatest potential for other Third World producers to build their own bicycle industries may lie in following the model of India, which began more than 50 years ago with mostly small-scale, family-run workshops. Today India produces some 8 million bicycles, 8 percent of the world total.[14]

As world automobile production surged upward during the sixties as part of the record economic expansion of that decade, it reached 23 million vehicles in 1969, nearly overtaking bicycle production at 25 million. Since then, the number of cars built has risen by about half, while bicycle production has almost quadrupled.[15] This is largely because, in the developing world, the number of people reaching the automobile-level of affluence over the last two decades has been relatively small compared with the number reaching the bicycle-level of affluence.

Bicycles have been seen as responsive to many of the problems facing societies everywhere, including urban air pollution, urban traffic congestion, and acid rain. Among those with sedentary life-styles, bicycle use for commuting and other short trips provides much-needed exercise. The steep upward swing in world total output since the mid-eighties is thus partly the result of both a fitness boom and an increase in bicycle commuting in industrial countries.

WORLD BICYCLE PRODUCTION, 1960–90

| YEAR | PRODUCTION (million) |
|------|------------|
| 1960 | 20 |
| 1961 | 20 |
| 1962 | 20 |
| 1963 | 20 |
| 1964 | 21 |
| 1965 | 21 |
| 1966 | 22 |
| 1967 | 23 |
| 1968 | 24 |
| 1969 | 25 |
| 1970 | 36 |
| 1971 | 39 |
| 1972 | 46 |
| 1973 | 52 |
| 1974 | 52 |
| 1975 | 43 |
| 1976 | 47 |
| 1977 | 49 |
| 1978 | 51 |
| 1979 | 54 |
| 1980 | 62 |
| 1981 | 65 |
| 1982 | 69 |
| 1983 | 74 |
| 1984 | 76 |
| 1985 | 79 |
| 1986 | 84 |
| 1987 | 98 |
| 1988 | 105 |
| 1989 | 95 |
| 1990 (est) | 95 |

SOURCES: UN, *The Growth of World Industry 1969 Edition,* Vol. II (New York: 1971); UN, *Yearbooks of Industrial Statistics 1979 and 1989 Editions,* Vol. II (New York: 1981 and 1991); 1990 figure, Worldwatch Institute estimate.

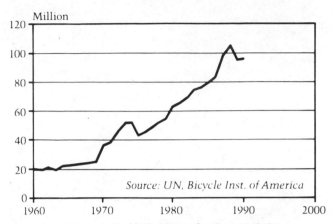

Figure 1: **World Bicycle Production, 1960–91**

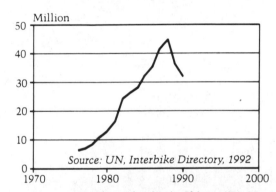

Figure 2: **Bicycle Production in China, 1976–90**

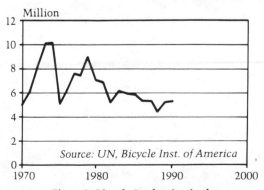

Figure 3: **Bicycle Production in the United States, 1970–90**

# Social
## Trends

# Population Growth Sets Record                    Lester R. Brown

World population grew in 1991 by a record 92 million, pushing the global total to 5.4 billion. (See Figures 1 and 2.) In effect, the world added the population-equivalent of Belgium, Denmark, the Netherlands, Norway, and the United Kingdom. Eighty-four million of the new arrivals live in the Third World.[1]

The 1991 population increase was the result of an excess of births, reported at 143 million, over deaths of 51 million. India was the principal contributor, adding 17 million, compared with China's 16 million. In the western hemisphere, Brazil, adding nearly 3 million, exceeded the U.S. natural increase of just over 2 million. Egypt, Ethiopia, and Nigeria each added more people than did all of Western Europe combined.[2]

The fastest growing regions are Africa and the Middle East, each expanding at about 3 percent a year, and each with a particular set of population-related issues.[3] In Africa, with the fastest population growth of any continent in history, per capita grain production has fallen nearly 20 percent since 1970, forcing the continent to import heavily.[4] After a generation of unprecedented population growth in the strife-ridden Middle East, severe water shortages are now emerging, raising the prospect that water could rival religion and oil as a source of conflict within the region.

At the other end of the spectrum, population growth in Europe, excluding the former Soviet Union, at 0.2 percent a year has brought the region close to population stability. Prominent among countries with stable populations that are not growing are Germany, Italy, and the United Kingdom. Altogether the group of countries at or near zero population growth includes roughly 500 million people, or 9 percent of the world's total population.[5]

Rapid population growth is such a recent historical phenomenon that we have difficulty grasping its dimensions and effects. Those born before the middle of this century have seen the number of people in the world double to more than 5 billion.[6] The environmental effects of adding 2.5 billion people are highly visible, especially in the Third World. They can be seen in the loss of tree cover, devastation of grasslands, soil erosion, crowding, poverty, land hunger, water

pollution, and the swelling streams of environmental refugees.

With the agricultural frontiers having disappeared, continuing population growth means the earth's finite resources, such as cropland, grasslands, and fresh water, are divided among an ever larger number of people. Partly as a result of these trends, the World Bank reports that per capita incomes fell during the eighties in at least 40 countries, containing more than 800 million people.[7] In virtually all of these, population is growing rapidly.

The sharp drops in annual additions to world population in 1960, 1961, and 1962 were the result of massive famine in China. The disruption that followed the ill-conceived "great leap" forward in 1958 led to a precipitous fall in food production. With the government unwilling to turn to the outside world for help, an estimated 30 million Chinese starved to death over the next few years.[8] This increase in deaths, combined with a hunger-induced drop in births in China, was so extensive that it dramatically slowed world population growth for a few years.

During the seventies, world population growth showed signs of levelling off, but efforts to slow growth then lost momentum, and in the mid-eighties, it climbed sharply. In part, this may have been the result of U.S. withdrawal of financial support from the U.N. Population Fund and the International Planned Parenthood Federation, the principal international sources of family planning assistance, allegedly because they were supporting abortion programs.[9] The effect of this action was a denial of family planning services to millions of women. Some believe that the increasing number of unwanted pregnancies and abortions in many developing countries may be caused in part by this policy.[10]

Fertility is now falling, albeit slowly, almost everywhere. Yet as many as 300 million couples still lack access to the services they need to plan their families.[11] The question is whether the transition to small families will move quickly enough to avoid rising death rates, nature's check on population growth.

## WORLD POPULATION, TOTAL AND ANNUAL INCREASE, 1950–91

| YEAR | POPULATION (billion) | INCREASE (million) |
|------|------|------|
| 1950 | 2.565 | |
| 1951 | 2.603 | 38 |
| 1952 | 2.645 | 42 |
| 1953 | 2.691 | 46 |
| 1954 | 2.739 | 48 |
| 1955 | 2.790 | 51 |
| 1956 | 2.843 | 53 |
| 1957 | 2.899 | 56 |
| 1958 | 2.955 | 57 |
| 1959 | 3.008 | 52 |
| 1960 | 3.050 | 42 |
| 1961 | 3.091 | 41 |
| 1962 | 3.148 | 57 |
| 1963 | 3.218 | 70 |
| 1964 | 3.290 | 72 |
| 1965 | 3.359 | 69 |
| 1966 | 3.429 | 70 |
| 1967 | 3.499 | 70 |
| 1968 | 3.571 | 72 |
| 1969 | 3.646 | 75 |
| 1970 | 3.721 | 76 |
| 1971 | 3.800 | 78 |
| 1972 | 3.877 | 78 |
| 1973 | 3.954 | 77 |
| 1974 | 4.030 | 76 |
| 1975 | 4.104 | 74 |
| 1976 | 4.177 | 73 |
| 1977 | 4.250 | 73 |
| 1978 | 4.323 | 73 |
| 1979 | 4.399 | 76 |
| 1980 | 4.476 | 77 |
| 1981 | 4.553 | 78 |
| 1982 | 4.634 | 80 |
| 1983 | 4.714 | 80 |
| 1984 | 4.794 | 80 |
| 1985 | 4.876 | 81 |
| 1986 | 4.959 | 83 |
| 1987 | 5.047 | 88 |
| 1988 | 5.136 | 89 |
| 1989 | 5.226 | 90 |
| 1990 | 5.317 | 90 |
| 1991 (est) | 5.409 | 92 |

SOURCE: Bureau of the Census data in USDA, *World Population by Country and Region, 1990* (Washington, D.C.: 1990).

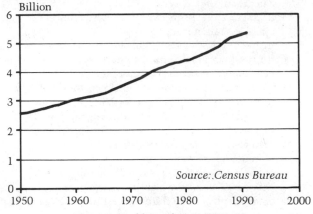

**Figure 1: World Population, 1950–91**

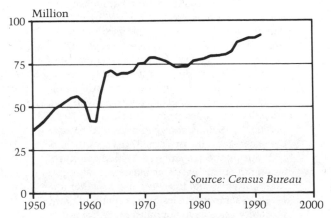

**Figure 2: Annual Addition to World Population, 1950–91**

77

# Infant Mortality Declining
Hal Kane

The infant mortality rate—the number of children per 1,000 births who die before one year of age—has fallen from 155 worldwide in 1950 to 63 in 1991.[1] (See Figure 1.) The lowest level ever, this follows a long-term historical decline that has accelerated over the last half-century.

The principal causes of reductions in infant mortality are increased access to immunizations for children, clean water for drinking and washing, sanitation, improved nutrition, and increased maternal literacy and education.

In the late seventies, immunization reached only about 10 percent of the developing world's children. During the eighties, however, rates increased substantially: from an estimated 27 percent coverage of children by immunizations for diphtheria, whooping cough, and tetanus in 1981, the 1990 rate reached 85 percent. For measles, the share went from 18 percent in 1981 to 79 percent in 1990. UNICEF reports that measles vaccinations alone now prevent 1.9 million child deaths every year. Yet 800,000 vaccine-preventable child deaths are still occurring among those who do not receive vaccinations.[2]

Female literacy and infant mortality are closely related. As the former goes up, the latter comes down. Among the poorest countries, women's literacy has improved from 8 percent in 1970 to 24 percent in 1990. Among countries in the next income category, it rose from 37 percent to 60 percent during the same period.[3] These gains are among the principal determinants of falling infant mortality, and the continued low literacy levels in some countries helps explain why infant mortality rates have not fallen more quickly there.

Infant mortality in developing regions during the early nineties averages 70 deaths per 1,000 births, while in industrial regions it is only 12. (See Figures 2 and 3.) Among developing countries, Jamaica's rate is 16, while China's is 30, India's is 95, and Mali suffers the most, at 167 infant deaths per 1,000 births.[4]

Within countries as well, infant mortality rates can vary widely. In the United States, infant deaths in Alabama, Georgia, and South Carolina average 12 per 1,000 births compared with only 6 in Vermont and Wyoming.[5] In the largest cities, including the metropolitan areas of Chicago, Detroit, Washington, D.C., Atlanta, St. Louis, and Baltimore, the rates are around 12 deaths per 1,000 births, while the U.S. rate is 10.[6] And among groups of people, rates vary significantly: in 1988, infant mortality of U.S. black children was nearly 18 per 1,000 compared with 8 for white children.[7] In developing countries, regional differences can be even greater.

Infant survival depends largely on the health of mothers. Poor nutrition and disease among women are passed on to infants, elevating rates of mortality. Poor health or low status among mothers also reduces their ability to provide food, fuel, and water for children, to cook meals and wash clothes, to clean homes, and to earn incomes.

Reproductive tract infections, including sexually transmitted diseases such as syphilis, gonorrhea, chlamydia, and AIDS, are epidemic among women in developing countries and contribute heavily to infant mortality.[8] In some of the world's poorest regions, those diseases are holding back the downward trend in infant mortality.

Infant mortality and population growth are firmly tied together. Declining infant mortality often makes family planning acceptable, as parents feel secure that the desired number of children will survive infancy. When infants die, however, parents reduce the spacing between pregnancies in an effort to replace lost infants. Wherever infants survive, birth rates usually go down.

The countries with the lowest levels of infant mortality are typically the wealthiest countries. Japan has brought mortality down to just 4 deaths per 1,000 births. For Sweden and Finland, the rate is 6. Canada, Switzerland, the Netherlands, France, and Hong Kong have the next best records, at 7 deaths per 1,000 births.[9]

## INFANT MORTALITY RATES, 1950–55 THROUGH 1990–95

| PERIOD | WORLD (deaths per 1,000 births) |
|--------|--------|
| 1950–55 | 155 |
| 1955–60 | 139 |
| 1960–65 | 118 |
| 1965–70 | 102 |
| 1970–75 | 93 |
| 1975–80 | 86 |
| 1980–85 | 79 |
| 1985–90 | 70 |
| 1990–95 | 63 |

| PERIOD | DEVELOPING COUNTRIES |
|--------|--------|
| 1950–55 | 180 |
| 1955–60 | 163 |
| 1960–65 | 136 |
| 1965–70 | 116 |
| 1970–75 | 105 |
| 1975–80 | 97 |
| 1980–85 | 89 |
| 1985–90 | 78 |
| 1990–95 | 70 |

| PERIOD | INDUSTRIAL COUNTRIES |
|--------|--------|
| 1950–55 | 56 |
| 1955–60 | 41 |
| 1960–65 | 32 |
| 1965–70 | 26 |
| 1970–75 | 22 |
| 1975–80 | 19 |
| 1980–85 | 16 |
| 1985–90 | 15 |
| 1990–95 | 12 |

SOURCE: United Nations, *World Population Prospects 1990* (New York: 1991).

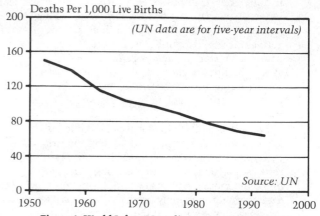

Deaths Per 1,000 Live Births

*(UN data are for five-year intervals)*

Source: UN

**Figure 1: World Infant Mortality, 1950–55 to 1990–95**

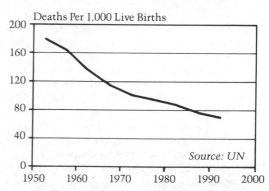

Deaths Per 1,000 Live Births

Source: UN

**Figure 2: Infant Mortality in Developing Countries, 1950–55 to 1990–95**

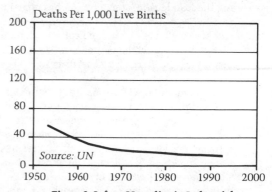

Deaths Per 1,000 Live Births

Source: UN

**Figure 3: Infant Mortality in Industrial Countries, 1950–55 to 1990–95**

# Cigarette Smoking Losing Favor    Lester R. Brown

In 1991, the world produced 5.4 trillion cigarettes, an average of 1,008 for each man, woman, and child on earth.[1] (See Figures 1 and 2.) Staggering though this number is, it is 1.5 percent below the historical high of 1,023 reached in 1988.[2] Declines in cigarette smoking in industrial societies appear to be overriding the growing popularity of this habit in many developing countries.

The steady growth in global consumption obscures widely disparate trends among countries. In China, which leads the world in total cigarettes smoked, consumption is rising steadily as more and more people can afford to smoke. With a government monopoly producing and marketing cigarettes throughout the country, smoking has soared.[3] This policy contrasts sharply with others of the government, which have been highly successful in improving health, giving China a life expectancy close to that of industrial societies.

By contrast, in the United States, which ranks second after China, consumption per person is falling precipitously.[4] (See Figure 3.) Most of the 38-percent drop in cigarettes smoked per U.S. adult since the historical high in 1963 has come over the last decade, as public awareness of the health effects has risen dramatically.

The fall in consumption began with the Surgeon General's report in 1964; by 1989, that office documented that 1,000 American smokers die each day from smoking-related illness.[5] During the last decade, consumption has gone into a free-fall as a steady flow of research reports on smoking's effects on human health have linked direct and indirect exposure to smoke to reduced birth weights, increased heart disease, and increases in several different cancers.

A University of California study estimates that 1,000 nonsmokers die each week in the United States from heart disease or cancer associated with smoking.[6] Recent evidence implicating cigarette smoking in 40 percent of all cancers has had a sobering effect.[7] California, the most populous state, has launched a highly successful $29-million-a-year antismoking campaign, financed by an increase in its cigarette tax.[8]

Restrictions on smoking in public places are also contributing to the rapid decline. A survey of 1,000 U.S. employers showed that 60 percent controlled smoking in the workplace and 25 percent banned it altogether.[9] Some firms go further, refusing to hire smokers. Domestic airline flights in the United States ban smoking entirely.[10] It is ironic that tobacco use is now declining most rapidly on the continent where it was first cultivated and where smoking originated.

In Canada, where public health officials are at the forefront of the efforts to discourage smoking, the average tax per pack, including both federal and provincial levies, is $3.76. This use of fiscal policy for health purposes pushed the average sale price per pack by late 1991 to $5.56, a level that is rapidly reducing cigarette use.[11]

As cigarette sales plummet in North America, U.S.-based manufacturers are shifting their efforts to the more prosperous regions of the Third World, such as East Asia, where less sophisticated consumers are more easily won over by the latest advertising techniques.[12]

As national governments recognize that cigarette smoking is raising health care costs, many are mobilizing to discourage smoking by prohibiting advertising, banning smoking in public places, and taxing cigarettes heavily. In Europe, the Scandinavian governments are among the leaders in discouraging smoking. In Norway, which has one of the world's most stringent policies, cigarette use has declined by nearly one fifth.[13] Many countries, including Hungary, Italy, Norway, and Poland, totally ban cigarette advertising.[14]

The antismoking movement is in the fledgling stage in Asia, but some governments are beginning to take strong steps. Hong Kong, for example, followed a 1990 ban on cigarette advertising on television with a tripling of the tax, pushing the price to $3 per pack.[15] In health-conscious Japan, the ranks of the antismoking movement are expanding.[16] And even China now has an embryonic antismoking movement.[17] As efforts to restrict cigarette smoking in this populous region gain momentum, the recent downturn in cigarettes produced per person worldwide could accelerate.

## WORLD CIGARETTE PRODUCTION, 1950–91

| YEAR | PRODUCTION (billion) | PER CAPITA (number of cigarettes) |
|------|------------|-----------|
| 1950 | 1,686 | 657 |
| 1951 | 1,733 | 666 |
| 1952 | 1,780 | 673 |
| 1953 | 1,827 | 679 |
| 1954 | 1,874 | 684 |
| 1955 | 1,921 | 689 |
| 1956 | 1,968 | 692 |
| 1957 | 2,015 | 695 |
| 1958 | 2,062 | 698 |
| 1959 | 2,108 | 701 |
| 1960 | 2,150 | 705 |
| 1961 | 2,140 | 692 |
| 1962 | 2,191 | 696 |
| 1963 | 2,300 | 715 |
| 1964 | 2,402 | 730 |
| 1965 | 2,564 | 763 |
| 1966 | 2,678 | 781 |
| 1967 | 2,689 | 769 |
| 1968 | 2,790 | 781 |
| 1969 | 2,924 | 802 |
| 1970 | 3,112 | 836 |
| 1971 | 3,165 | 833 |
| 1972 | 3,295 | 850 |
| 1973 | 3,481 | 880 |
| 1974 | 3,590 | 890 |
| 1975 | 3,742 | 912 |
| 1976 | 3,852 | 922 |
| 1977 | 4,019 | 946 |
| 1978 | 4,072 | 942 |
| 1979 | 4,214 | 958 |
| 1980 | 4,388 | 980 |
| 1981 | 4,541 | 997 |
| 1982 | 4,550 | 982 |
| 1983 | 4,547 | 965 |
| 1984 | 4,689 | 978 |
| 1985 | 4,855 | 998 |
| 1986 | 4,987 | 1,006 |
| 1987 | 5,128 | 1,016 |
| 1988 | 5,256 | 1,023 |
| 1989 | 5,286 | 1,011 |
| 1990 | 5,414 | 1,018 |
| 1991 | 5,450 | 1,008 |

SOURCES: Dan Stevens, USDA, FAS, unpublished printout, November 7, 1991; population from USDA; data for 1950 based on U.S. trend; 1951–58 numbers simple arithmetic extrapolations.

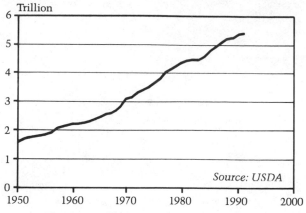

Figure 1: World Cigarette Production, 1950–91

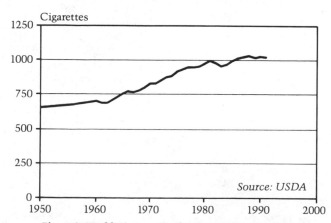

Figure 2: World Cigarette Production Per Person, 1950–91

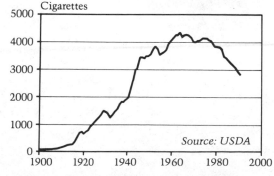

Figure 3: US Cigarette Consumption Per Person, 1900–91

# Military Trends

# Military Expenditures Falling                      Michael Renner

World military expenditures declined an estimated 6 percent in 1990, to about $935 billion (in 1990 dollars).[1] For four decades following World War II, only the sky seemed the limit—spending for wars and war preparation rose to an all-time high in 1987 of more than $1 trillion. The end of the cold war and dire economic straits, however, have combined to reduce military expenditures. (See Figure 1.)

Calculating global military expenditures is fraught with numerous uncertainties. Many countries keep military spending data secret. Due to deceptive accounting practices, off-budget financing, and barter of military imports, official figures often veil significant parts of these expenditures.[2] The figure presented here therefore illustrates the general trend rather than a precise set of numbers.

One particularly difficult case has been the former Soviet Union. Its system permitted the allocation of funds in excess of existing budgets, if necessary, through subsidies or deficit financing. Until 1989, official figures covered only expenses for personnel, construction, and maintenance, not weapons procurement or research and development.[3] Even with greater transparency, prices set administratively by Moscow's central bureaucracy rendered any set of estimates somewhat arbitrary.

Estimates of Soviet expenditures by the U.S. Central Intelligence Agency (CIA) appear to be too high and riddled with inconsistencies. By calculating what it would cost in dollars to replicate the Soviet military force in the United States, actual outlays were exaggerated.[4]

The Stockholm International Peace Research Institute (SIPRI) provides a more plausible estimate, translating ruble costs into dollars with the help of estimated purchasing power parities. SIPRI estimates that the Soviet Union spent $270 billion in 1989 and $248 billion in 1990, but it provides no data for 1986-88.[5] To arrive at global totals for these years, Soviet figures for this period have been calculated on the basis of the 1989 SIPRI figure and CIA-estimated annual percentage growth rates.[6]

Military spending in the former Soviet Union is now declining rapidly. In late January 1992, the Russian parliament approved a budget that slashes arms purchases by a staggering 85 percent compared with the 1991 level.[7]

U.S. national defense outlays peaked in 1989 at $315 billion, and fell to $287 billion in 1991 (in 1990 dollars).[8] The budget is certain to decline further during the nineties; the only questions are how far and how fast. President Bush has proposed only modest cuts,[9] and Pentagon plans for procuring a new generation of high-tech weapons may actually cause budgets to rise again later in the decade. Congressional leaders and former government officials have urged more substantial reductions.[10] (See Figure 2.)

The United States and the former Soviet Union together account for about 60 percent of global military expenditures. Europe is the third-largest spender. During the eighties, the global share accounted for by the Middle East, Africa, and Latin America declined, while that of Asia increased.

Among the world's 30 largest spenders, Canada, Italy, Japan, North and South Korea, Pakistan, Taiwan, Thailand, and Turkey registered hefty increases during the eighties. Malaysia is planning to quadruple its military budget. By contrast, Argentina, Brazil, Egypt, Indonesia, Iran, Israel, Libya, Poland, and Syria appear to have made substantial cuts.[11] Following a decade-long spending spree, India's military apparatus is now forced to tighten belts to tackle the country's budget and balance-of-payments imbalance.[12] In general, Third World military expenditures have fallen rapidly since 1984, principally as a result of severe economic crises.[13]

In China, meanwhile, a stunning reversal has taken place. Military spending was reduced throughout the eighties, the armed forces pared back, and many defense enterprises converted to civilian production.[14] But between 1989 and 1992, Chinese military expenditures have been increased by 50 percent, largely to reward the armed forces for crushing the prodemocracy movement.[15]

By the sheer size of their budgets, future trends in global military expenditures will be primarily shaped by developments in the United States and Russia. While many countries are now streamlining their armed forces and arms industries, they also seek to modernize them, putting a limit to how far military budgets will decline.

## WORLD MILITARY EXPENDITURES, 1950–90

| YEAR | EXPENDITURE (bill. 1990 dollars) |
|------|------------|
| 1950 | 230 |
| 1951 | 337 |
| 1952 | 432 |
| 1953 | 444 |
| 1954 | 399 |
| 1955 | 397 |
| 1956 | 397 |
| 1957 | 405 |
| 1958 | 399 |
| 1959 | 415 |
| 1960 | 408 |
| 1961 | 453 |
| 1962 | 495 |
| 1963 | 517 |
| 1964 | 511 |
| 1965 | 514 |
| 1966 | 561 |
| 1967 | 619 |
| 1968 | 658 |
| 1969 | 669 |
| 1970 | 658 |
| 1971 | 656 |
| 1972 | 663 |
| 1973 | 743 |
| 1974 | 766 |
| 1975 | 789 |
| 1976 | 800 |
| 1977 | 813 |
| 1978 | 837 |
| 1979 | 860 |
| 1980 | 867 |
| 1981 | 887 |
| 1982 | 940 |
| 1983 | 966 |
| 1984 | 984 |
| 1985 | 1,017 |
| 1986 | 1,021 |
| 1987 | 1,026 |
| 1988 | 1,021 |
| 1989 | 990 |
| 1990 | 934 |

SOURCES: *Bulletin of Peace Proposals,* No. 3–4, 1986; *SIPRI Yearbook 1991;* Worldwatch Institute estimates.

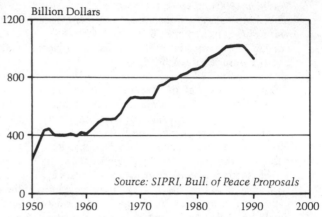

**Figure 1: World Military Expenditures, 1950–90**

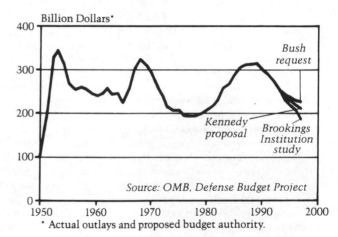

* Actual outlays and proposed budget authority.

**Figure 2: U.S. Military Expenditures, 1950–92, With Projections for 1993–97**

# Nuclear Arsenal Shrinking Michael Renner

Between 1990 and 1991, the number of strategic offensive warheads in the world's nuclear arsenal was reduced from some 23,700 to 19,200, a decline of 19 percent.[1] From the start of the nuclear age, the number of warheads grew rapidly, virtually unconstrained by arms control treaties. (See Figure 1.) At its peak in 1988, the global stockpile included almost 25,000 strategic warheads and more than 30,000 tactical ones (those that travel 3,000 miles or less). The United States and the former Soviet Union account for more than 95 percent of the global total.[2] (See Figure 2.)

This seemingly endless growth was reversed with the end of the cold war, reinforced by budgetary constraints and the revelation of pervasive health and safety problems in the superpowers' weapons production complexes.[3]

The 1987 Intermediate-Range Nuclear Forces Treaty resulted in the first small but real reductions in nuclear arsenals. The 1991 START Treaty will yield additional cuts. General Colin Powell, chairman of the U.S. Joint Chiefs of Staff, projects post-START strategic warheads at 9,500 for the United States; the corresponding number for the Commonwealth of Independent States might be around 7,000.[4]

Recent initiatives outside the framework of formal arms negotiations, prompted by growing domestic pressure for more weapons cuts and by fears that the disintegration of the Soviet Union might accelerate nuclear proliferation, will slash the arsenals of mass destruction much more deeply.

President Bush's pledge to withdraw all remaining ground-based and naval U.S. tactical nuclear weapons will lead to the destruction of some 2,400 out of a total of 7,147 tactical warheads and to an unspecified number being put in storage.[5] In addition, NATO leaders decided to withdraw from Europe about half the 1,400 U.S. air-launched tactical nuclear weapons.[6] President Gorbachev quickly matched the Bush offer, offering to destroy at least 4,800 warheads and to withdraw another 3,400.[7]

Predicated on Russian consent to ban all land-based multiple-warhead missiles, Bush also offered a plan that would reduce U.S. strategic warheads to 4,700 and would leave Russia with a total of about 4,400. (The other states emerging from the old Soviet Union will become denuclea-

rized.) In response, Russian President Yeltsin challenged the United States to accept a limit of about 3,000 strategic warheads each. Reconciling these two plans, the two countries both agreed in June 1992 to reduce their arsenals to 3,000-3,500 warheads by the year 2003.[8]

Meanwhile, the other self-acknowledged nuclear powers—Britain, France, and China—have offered only token measures. In fact, the combined total of these countries' nuclear arms is projected to grow from nearly 1,500 warheads now to 2,000 within a few years.[9]

In the late eighties, the U.S. government had the capacity to produce or modify some 3,500-4,000 warheads per year.[10] Since July 1990, however, no new nuclear warhead has been manufactured and no new programs are on the books.[11] In Russia, the manufacturing of some nuclear weapons components is apparently continuing.[12] The production of weapons-grade fissile materials has slowed considerably, though stockpiles remain huge. The United States halted plutonium production in 1988. In the former Soviet Union, production continues at 6 of 14 reactors that were operating in the mid-eighties.[13]

The number of nuclear weapons tests has declined dramatically. (See Figure 3.) The former Soviet Union closed its major test ground in Kazakhstan; Russia is observing a unilateral one-year testing moratorium, but might resume testing if the United States continues to reject a test ban.[14] In April 1992, France suspended its testing for at least eight months, and possibly longer.[15]

The United States and Russia are now planning to halt or sharply curtail the production of strategic bombers, ballistic missiles, and cruise missiles. The stage is set for a dramatic decrease in the world's nuclear arsenal. But it will still contain enough firepower to annihilate life on earth, and none of the nuclear powers is publicly contemplating the eventual abolition of nuclear weapons.

GLOBAL NUCLEAR ARSENAL, 1950–91

| YEAR | STRATEGIC OFFENSIVE NUCLEAR WARHEADS |
|------|--------------------------------------|
| 1950 | 400 |
| 1951 | 569 |
| 1952 | 660 |
| 1953 | 878 |
| 1954 | 1,418 |
| 1955 | 1,755 |
| 1956 | 2,207 |
| 1957 | 2,562 |
| 1958 | 2,836 |
| 1959 | 2,849 |
| 1960 | 3,586 |
| 1961 | 3,696 |
| 1962 | 3,928 |
| 1963 | 4,408 |
| 1964 | 5,159 |
| 1965 | 5,312 |
| 1966 | 5,801 |
| 1967 | 6,481 |
| 1968 | 6,737 |
| 1969 | 6,776 |
| 1970 | 7,431 |
| 1971 | 8,796 |
| 1972 | 10,508 |
| 1973 | 11,971 |
| 1974 | 12,514 |
| 1975 | 13,471 |
| 1976 | 14,355 |
| 1977 | 15,300 |
| 1978 | 16,856 |
| 1979 | 17,889 |
| 1980 | 18,632 |
| 1981 | 19,543 |
| 1982 | 19,977 |
| 1983 | 20,655 |
| 1984 | 21,693 |
| 1985 | 22,640 |
| 1986 | 23,133 |
| 1987 | 24,157 |
| 1988 | 24,545 |
| 1989 | 24,205 |
| 1990 | 23,718 |
| 1991 | 19,165 |

SOURCE: *SIPRI Yearbook 1992.*

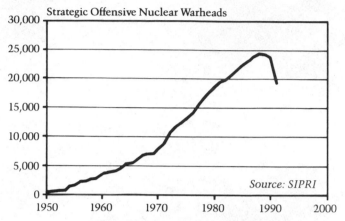

Strategic Offensive Nuclear Warheads

Source: SIPRI

**Figure 1: Global Nuclear Arsenal, 1950–91**

Strategic Offensive Nuclear Warheads

United States    Soviet Union

Source: SIPRI

**Figure 2: U.S. and Soviet Nuclear Arsenals, 1950–91**

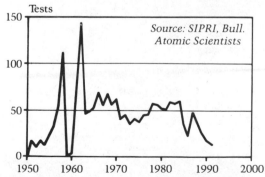

Tests

Source: SIPRI, Bull. Atomic Scientists

**Figure 3: Nuclear Warhead Tests, 1950–91 \***

\* Does not reflect an additional 87 French and Soviet tests unidentified by year that took place during the period covered.

Part **TWO**

# Special Features

# Environmental Features

# Birds Fast Disappearing

**Howard Youth**

Some 9,000 bird species currently live in the world's forests, grasslands, deserts, wetlands, and other habitats. Through millions of years of evolution, each species has evolved a distinct set of living requirements. From a bee-sized hummingbird to an eight-foot-tall ostrich, each depends on adequate amounts of habitat in which to breed, feed, and rest. Extreme alteration to a particular habitat often elicits a quick drop or rise in that area's bird populations. Because of this sensitivity, and their high visibility, birds are barometers of environmental change.

Today, about 1,000 bird species—more than 11 percent—are at risk of extinction, while about 70 percent, or 6,300 species, are in decline.[1] Habitat destruction is by far the most sinister threat to the majority of these birds, and to the other animals and plants that share their habitat. As the last large pockets of tropical forest—home to at least 3,500 bird species—fall to satisfy human needs for food, lumber, and minerals, even the freedom of flight cannot save birds.[2]

Throughout history, human settlement has left behind a trail of bird extinctions. A wave of bird die-offs in Hawaii and other Pacific islands, for instance, resulted from overhunting by Polynesians even before Captain James Cook arrived in 1778.[3] Since then, exotic species introduced by western settlers have threatened most of the islands' remaining endemic species.

Similar effects have been felt on the mainland. From the mid-nineteenth century through the early twentieth, for example, virtually all large stands of virgin forest in the southeastern United States fell to loggers, while hunters took aim at birds for the plume trade and urban meat markets. By the twenties, the once-widespread ivory-billed woodpecker, Carolina parakeet, and passenger pigeon had become only museum memories.[4]

Because they are easier to survey than other animals, birds are often accurate indicators of overall imbalances in a habitat that affect other species. The U.S. battle over the northern subspecies of spotted owl is, therefore, really over the future of old-growth forests in general, since not only the owl but also dozens of other species, from the red-backed vole to the Pacific yew tree, are in danger.

Judging from the health of certain avian populations, the health of the world's ecosystems is faltering. Many neotropical migrants, a group of about 150 songbirds, hawks, and shorebirds that winter in Central and South America but breed in North America, have shown alarming drops in population over the last 10-15 years (see Table 1), due primarily to deforestation in both the northern and southern parts of their ranges.[5]

Common British woodland and farmland birds have been declining since the end of World War II, as 45 percent of the forests and 22 percent of the "natural boundary" hedgerows were plowed down to increase cropland size for larger, more modern machinery.[6]

But birds do not reside only in forests, and their declines have been striking in other habitats as well. The disappearance of wetlands, mainly from conversion to farmland or industrial areas, has been marked by a sharp decline in duck species in North America as well as other water-dependent species. Overall, duck populations in

TABLE 1: DECLINES IN SOME WIDESPREAD NEOTROPICAL MIGRANTS, 1978–87

| SPECIES | ANNUAL DECLINE (percent) |
| --- | --- |
| Yellow-billed Cuckoo | 5 |
| Wood Thrush | 4 |
| Black-throated Green Warbler | 3.1 |
| Northern Oriole | 2.9 |
| Canada Warbler | 2.7 |
| Northern Parula Warbler | 2.1 |
| Kentucky Warbler | 1.6 |
| Ovenbird | 1 |

SOURCE: Chandler S. Robbins et al., "Population Declines in North American Birds that Migrate to the Neotropics," Proceedings of the National Academy of Sciences, Washington, D.C., June 29, 1989.

the "prairie pothole" regions of the central United States and the southern half of Canada have dropped more than 30 percent since 1955.[7]

The conversion of tidal flats in Japan to land-fills, docking areas, and leisure resorts has severely reduced migrating bird concentration points.[8] Along the U.S. East Coast, intense beach-side recreation has eliminated from their only habitat the Snowy Plover (now listed as threatened) and other species, from ghost crabs to erosion-fighting beach grasses.[9]

Birds are also reacting to changes humans cause in the earth's chemistry. High levels of selenium resulting from chemical-laden agricultural water that washed into California's Kesterson National Wildlife Refuge and a number of other important wetlands resulted in failed nesting—due to embryo mortality and birth defects—of large numbers of common waterbirds.[10]

Concentrations of organochlorine and heavy metals found in the tissue of shorebirds feeding in wetlands near Texas industrial sites indicate widespread danger of toxic contamination in wetlands.[11] This buildup is an even greater danger to predators, which accumulate higher concentrations of toxins as they feed on contaminated shorebirds.

The population of the dipper, a semiaquatic bird that lives and feeds in rapidly flowing streams, has declined in Wales where pine plantations have replaced the native oak woods and made the water too acidic. The birds' increased scarcity is probably due to the fact that their prey, aquatic insects, cannot tolerate boosted acidity.[12]

Pesticides are among the most difficult to track of all the dangers to birds. Numerous birds have been killed by the misuse of the insecticide Furadan on a variety of crops. In five incidents alone,

this pesticide killed more than 5,000 ducks and geese that were feeding on or near sprayed alfalfa.[13] Sprayings for locusts in Africa in 1986 and 1987 reportedly killed most birds unlucky enough to fall under the spray.[14]

In the sixties, sharp declines in brown pelicans, ospreys, peregrine falcons, and bald eagles in North America led to a ban there of DDT, which caused birds to lay eggs with thinned shells that cracked prematurely during incubation. Since the ban, all four species have rebounded in varying degrees. Pesticide residues found in birds of prey in Africa and South America, where DDT is still widely used, indicate that the pesticide is taking a similar toll in the Third World.[15]

Even harder to trace is the effect human activities have on the genetic makeup of species. As a species becomes rarer, its genetic pool narrows, reducing the genetic variability and health of species.

The ways in which humans coexist or choose to ignore other species will determine the biological diversity of the future. Currently, the most concentrated threat to bird—and other—species is in "biological hotspots," where unusually high numbers of endemic species, those unique to one location, are clustered in small areas.[16] Recent studies of bird distribution reveal that 20 percent of all bird species occur in only 2 percent of the world's land.[17] Most of this falls in tropical countries, the majority of which are still poorly studied and currently lack effective conservation programs.

The diminished health and disappearance of bird species worldwide indicates an environment at risk. Increasingly, it is becoming clear that the welfare of these winged indicators is inextricably tied to ours.

# Forests Shrinking at Record Rate — Lester R. Brown

When agriculture began, the earth had a rich mantle of forest and open woodland covering some 6.2 billion hectares. Over the centuries, a combination of land clearing for crop production, commercial timber harvesting, cattle ranching, and fuelwood gathering has shrunk the earth's forests to some 4.2 billion hectares—a third less than existed in preagricultural times.[1]

For centuries, this reduction in the earth's biological stock hindered human progress little, if at all. Indeed, the clearing of trees to expand food production and the harvesting of forest products was part and parcel of economic and social development. But trees quite literally form the roots of many natural systems. With the inexorable march of deforestation, the ecological integrity of many areas is disintegrating—causing severe soil loss, aggravating droughts and floods, disrupting water supplies, and reducing land productivity.

Trees are also a vital component of the survival economy of the rural poor. Hundreds of millions of people rely on gathered wood to cook their meals and heat their homes. For them, lack of access to wood translates into reduced living standards and, in some cases, directly into malnutrition. In addition, trees and soils play a crucial role in the global cycling of carbon, the importance of which has been magnified by the emergence of carbon dioxide-induced climate change as arguably the most threatening environmental problem of modern times.

Despite growing public concern over tropical deforestation, the rate for forest loss has accelerated over the last decade. In 1982, the U.N. Food and Agriculture Organization reported that the world was losing some 11 million hectares of tropical forest per year.[2] A decade later, it places the annual loss at 17 million hectares.[3] Fortunately, reforestation is also proceeding somewhat faster than official estimates suggest. Spontaneous tree planting by villagers around farm fields, as windbreaks, or along roadways is frequently not counted.

Nonetheless, the loss of forest cover in tropical countries remains rampant. Conversion of forest to cropland and rangeland is by far the leading direct cause. Population growth, inequitable land distribution, and the expansion of export agriculture have greatly reduced the area of cropland available for subsistence farming, forcing many peasants to clear virgin forest to grow food.

Population pressures have also transformed fuelwood collection into an unsustainable practice. It is an agent of forest destruction primarily in the arid woodlands of Africa, where population density is high and the natural growth rate of vegetation is low, and around large cities of Asia and Africa, where concentrated demand overtaxes available tree stock. (See Table 1.) Recent Landsat data show that in less than a decade, forest cover within 100 kilometers of India's major cities dropped by 15 percent or more; Delhi lost a staggering 60 percent.[4]

Consumer demand in temperate countries fos-

## TABLE 1: SHARE OF TOTAL ENERGY USE PROVIDED BY WOOD, SELECTED COUNTRIES, EARLY EIGHTIES

| COUNTRY | WOOD SHARE OF TOTAL ENERGY USE (percent) |
|---|---|
| **Africa** | |
| Burkina Faso | 96 |
| Kenya | 71 |
| Malawi | 93 |
| Nigeria | 82 |
| Sudan | 74 |
| Tanzania | 92 |
| **Asia** | |
| China | > 25[1] |
| India | 33 |
| Indonesia | 50 |
| Nepal | 94 |
| **Latin America** | |
| Brazil | 20 |
| Costa Rica | 33 |
| Nicaragua | 50 |
| Paraguay | 64 |

[1]Includes agricultural wastes and dung in addition to wood and charcoal.
SOURCE: Worldwatch Institute, based on various sources.

TABLE 2: PER CAPITA PAPER AND PAPER BOARD USE, SELECTED COUNTRIES AND REGIONS, 1988

| COUNTRY OR REGION | CONSUMPTION (kilograms/year) |
|---|---|
| United States | 317 |
| Sweden | 311 |
| Canada | 247 |
| Japan | 204 |
| Norway | 151 |
| Soviet Union | 35 |
| Latin America | 25 |
| China | 12 |
| Africa | 5 |
| India | 2 |

SOURCE: Greenpeace, *The Greenpeace Guide to Paper* (Vancouver: 1990).

ters tropical forest depletion as well. (See Table 2.) Industrial countries' appetite for tropical hardwoods has encouraged many Third World governments, notably in Southeast Asia, to "mine" their forests to earn vital foreign exchange. As loggers selectively fell commercially valuable tree species—which sometimes account for less than 5 percent of any given hectare—they often destroy between 30 and 60 percent of unwanted trees as well.[5]

In Latin America, it is the lure of cattle ranching, particularly in Brazil and Central America, that is destroying vast areas of forest. Between 1961 and 1978, pasture in Central America expanded 53 percent while forests and woodlands declined 39 percent.[6]

Efforts to slow deforestation certainly deserve redoubled support. But even if forest clearing miraculously ceased today, millions of hectares of trees would still have to be planted to meet future needs for fuelwood, paper, and lumber; to stabilize soil and water resources; and to mitigate the buildup of atmospheric carbon dioxide. This latter need gives industrial countries sound reason to step up support for tree planting in the Third World.

Pressures on temperate forests have waned following several centuries of clearing for agriculture. Despite strong demand for paper, lumber, and other forest products, forest cover in most European countries is now fairly stable. In some, it has even been increasing as marginal agricultural land reverts to woodland and as conscious efforts are made to plant trees. Since the early sixties, U.K. government and private plantings have increased net forest cover an average of 30,000-40,000 hectares per year.[7] In France, forest area has risen substantially from its historic low of 14 percent in 1789; about a quarter of the country is now forested.[8] Unfortunately, chemical stresses from air pollution and acid rain today place many European forests at risk. In some countries, including Czechoslovakia, Germany, and Switzerland, close to half or more of all forests are showing signs of damage linked to air pollutants.[9]

As in Europe, forest cover in the contiguous United States was comparatively stable during most of this century, following the loss of 136 million hectares between 1630 and 1920. During the sixties and seventies, however, forest area declined as widening grain and soybean export markets encouraged conversion of forest to cropland and as urban and industrial development encroached on woodland. By 1982, forests covered 233 million hectares of the contiguous states—a 10-percent drop from 1963, and less than existed in 1920, the previous low point.[10]

In the Third World, nothing in prospect suggests that forest cover will stabilize anytime soon, as it has in many industrial countries. The forces behind deforestation remain strong, and planting efforts are woefully inadequate to reverse the loss of tree cover.

Adapted and updated from
Sandra Postel and Lori Heise,
"Reforesting the Earth," in
*State of the World 1988*

# U.S. Soil Erosion Cut                                    Lester R. Brown

Between 1985 and 1990, U.S. farmers cut their losses of topsoil from wind and water erosion by more than one third.[1] This reduction, the result of an innovative national program incorporated in the 1985 farm bill, is the first major breakthrough in the effort to stem the heavy worldwide losses of soil.

On close to a third of the world's cropland, soil erosion now exceeds the natural rate of new soil formation.[2] As the world demand for food continues to rise, farmers are forced onto marginal land that is highly erodible and they adopt more-intensive cropping practices that accelerate soil erosion.

Even agriculturally advanced countries such as the United States can experience heavy losses of topsoil. The U.S. Department of Agriculture estimated in 1977 that U.S. soil losses may have matched those at the Dust Bowl's peak.[3] But this time erosion was caused less by wind than by water, and was concentrated not in the western plains but in the Corn Belt and the South.

The three other leading food producers—India, China, and the former Soviet Union, which with the United States account for half of world food output—are also losing topsoil at an unsustainable rate. India estimates that 6 billion tons of topsoil wash or blow away each year from some 140 million hectares of cropland, more than double U.S. losses on roughly the same cropland area.[4] In China, the Hwang Ho, or Yellow River, deposits 1.16 billion tons of soil into the Yellow Sea each year; springtime dust storms in northern China often bring automobile and airline traffic to a halt.[5] In Russia, heavy soil losses may be compounding other more obvious structural problems in agriculture.[6]

The only major food-producing country to respond to the erosion threat is the United States. Twice in this century it has faced the economic and environmental ravages of escalating soil losses, first in the Dust Bowl era of the thirties and then again beginning in the late seventies. In both cases, creative policies and decisive action averted disaster.

The Dust Bowl, though triggered by the drought, resulted from the overplowing and continuous cropping that removed too much of the land's protective vegetation. In the spring of 1935, Congress responded by passing the Soil Conservation Act.[7] This created the Soil Conservation Service, which actively assisted farmers in planting rows of trees for windbreaks, fallowing land, and strip-cropping.[8] These and other government-assisted conservation practices brought the Dust Bowl crisis under control within a few years, restoring the land and economy of the Great Plains.

But even as the dust clouds were disappearing, the seeds of another crisis were being sown. Growing overseas demand for U.S. farm products and the availability of cheap chemical fertilizer led farmers to dispense with traditional rotations that included nitrogen-fixing legumes, such as clover, and to turn to continuous cropping of corn. But crop rotations including legumes not only fix nitrogen, they also hold the soil in place. Land on a test plot in Missouri that was losing three tons of soil per acre in a corn-wheat-clover rotation began losing 10 tons a year when it was planted continuously in wheat, and more than 19 tons when planted continuously in corn.[9] Several studies showed that for every inch of topsoil lost, wheat and corn yields typically decline 6 percent.[10]

During the early seventies, U.S. farmers planted just under 150 million acres (61 million hectares) of grain per year, but by 1977 they were planting 180 million acres, an increase of

TABLE 1: UNITED STATES: PROGRESS IN REDUCING SOIL EROSION FROM CROPLANDS, 1986–90, WITH PROJECTIONS TO 1995

| SOIL LOSS | MILLION TONS |
|---|---|
| Excessive soil loss in 1985 | 1,620 |
| Reduction, 1986–90 | − 550 |
| Projected reduction, 1991–95 | − 400 |
| Remaining excessive soil erosion | 670 |

SOURCE: USDA, ERS, *Agricultural Resources: Cropland, Water, and Conservation Situation and Outlook Report,* Washington, D.C., September 1990.

more than one fifth as they responded to world food shortages.[11] As production climbed, so did soil erosion. In 1985, soil erosion losses from cropland in excess of natural soil formation were estimated at 1.6 billion tons.[12]

In the early eighties, a coalition of environmental groups and soil conservation professionals launched a new approach. They helped shape the soil conservation section of the Food Security Act, the most ambitious soil-conservation initiative ever undertaken by any country.[13] While it retained traditional programs to curb surpluses, the Food Security Act contained two key provisions designed to reduce soil erosion. The Conservation Reserve Program, which covers 1986-95, has paid farmers to plant highly erodible cropland in grass or trees under 10-year contracts—with a total of 14 million hectares planted through 1991.[14] By paying farmers to take this land out of production, the program helped control excess production and cut the national loss of topsoil by 550 million tons, roughly one third.[15] (See Table 1.)

The second provision, designed to control erosion on the remaining 47 million hectares of highly erodible land, required farmers to develop a comprehensive soil-conserving farm plan by 1990 and to fully implement it by 1995 or lose all farm program benefits, including price supports,

low interest loans, and crop insurance.[16] The conservation practices incorporated in these farm plans include shifting to less intensive cropping patterns and to minimal tillage or no-till agricultural practices. If successfully implemented, this second phase could cut soil losses by an additional 400 million tons, making a total reduction in soil losses of nearly two thirds within a decade.[17]

This U.S. achievement is noteworthy for two reasons. First, it helps secure the long-term productivity of the world's breadbasket, which accounts for one sixth of world grain output.[18] Second, it provides a model for other countries.

With a food-production capacity that far exceeds domestic needs, the United States found it relatively painless to convert highly erodible cropland to grass or trees. Developing countries filled with hungry people will be hard-pressed to rescue rapidly eroding land by converting it to less-intensive uses, such as growing firewood. The question, however, is not whether the highly erodible cropland eventually will be abandoned, for it will be once the topsoil is gone. The real question is whether farmers can incorporate fodder and firewood production into an agroforestry plan that will stabilize their soils before they are left with only wasteland.

# Steel Recycling Rising Slowly

**Hal Kane**

In the mid-eighties, roughly one fourth of world steel output came from recycled scrap.[1] In the United States, a leader in steel recycling, 46 percent of 1990 steel production came from this source: 97 million tons of new raw steel were produced using 45 million tons of scrap.[2] (See Figure 1.)

The production of steel from raw ore consumes vast amounts of energy and is a major source of pollution and environmental disruption. In the mid-eighties, steelmaking consumed 15 percent of all commercial energy used in Japan and the Soviet Union, more than 9 percent of all energy used in Brazil, and some 6 percent of world energy use.[3]

Recycling of steel cuts energy use drastically, as steel produced from secondary materials consumes only one fourth to half as much energy as that made from primary materials. Moreover, producing steel from scrap reduces air pollution 85 percent, water pollution 76 percent, water use 40 percent, and mining wastes 97 percent.[4]

With the growth in the late eighties of U.S. markets for scrap steel, the number of people employed in the steel scrap industry as dealers, brokers, and processors grew from 87,400 in 1986 to 113,000 in 1990, increasing every year.[5] While using far less energy and generating relatively little pollution, producing steel from scrap creates more jobs than doing so from ore does.

Efficiency rates in steel production vary widely among countries, largely according to the amount of recycling done. Italy and Spain rank highest in energy efficiency in steel manufacturing because they are major recyclers. They use only 18 gigajoules of energy to produce a ton of steel, a rate they accomplish through use of the electric arc or "recycling" furnace that can use entirely scrap metal.[6]

The former Soviet Union, one of the big five steel producers (along with the United States, Japan, China, and Germany), recycles little steel and relies heavily on the use of virgin iron ores and inefficient open hearth furnaces, which can not use more than 45 percent scrap. Steel production there requires 31 gigajoules per ton—some 70 percent more than in Italy or Spain.[7] The open hearth furnace was used for 87 percent of steel production in the United States as recently as 1960, but now it accounts for less than 8 percent of U.S. output.[8]

In Eastern Europe, this traditional technology supplies 55-60 percent of production, while the electric arc furnace, which now dominates in the United States and Western Europe, provides less than 13 percent.[9] China and India also still rely heavily on the open hearth furnace, using more than twice as much energy per ton of steel produced as in the most efficient countries.

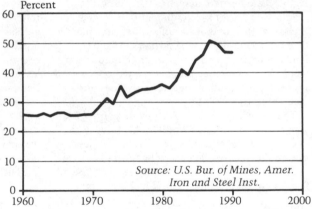

Figure 1: Share of U.S. Raw Steel Produced from Scrap, 1960–90

In the United States, a group of small steel recycling companies using electric arc minimills more than doubled their capacity between 1975 and 1985, a time when the U.S. steel industry was shrinking by almost one fifth.[10] Highly competitive because of their lower costs, minimills are projected to account for about 40 percent of U.S. raw steel production by the end of the nineties.[11]

In the mid-eighties, electric arc furnaces generated over 53 percent of raw steel production in Italy, almost 56 percent in Spain, 51 percent in Sweden, 55 percent in Argentina, and 45 percent in Mexico.[12] Not all that production was from recycled materials, because primary products can also be used, but those high rates indicate both high potential and actual recycling. The Development Centre of the Organisation for Economic

Co-operation and Development projects that electric arc furnaces will account for 49 percent of world steel output by the end of the nineties.[13]

Especially in the United States, the small minimills are able to adapt quickly to new technology, and are efficient and flexible. Traditionally, steel mills concentrated in areas where coal and iron ore are found in close proximity, such as the United Kingdom, the Ruhr Valley in Europe, or the Pittsburgh region in the United States. In contrast, minimills and other plants with electric arc furnaces are widely dispersed. This has allowed the smaller mills access to scrap materials and to local markets not available to larger firms, and has reduced transportation costs substantially.

Minimills typically produce a narrow range of products, and both the location and product mix of plants are designed to meet specific market requirements. Most of the companies produce carbon bars, reinforcing bars, structural shapes, wire rods, or tubular products. These mills also have been able to take on new types of materials and use new processes. For example, between 1989 and 1992, the number of North American markets for scrap from steel cans tripled, as flexible mills were increasingly able to find technology to use the cans.[14]

Worldwide, however, the growth of steel recycling may face limits caused by impurities in scrap metal that make recycled metals brittle. Copper, especially, is frequently mixed in with scrap metals, such as recycled automobile parts, and metals produced with it and other extraneous elements can only be made into a limited group of products, such as reinforcing bars.[15] As a result, minimills and other recycling technologies often do not compete directly with more traditional basic oxygen furnaces because they cannot make the same products.

Such barriers to the growth of recycling can be overcome if industry focuses more on the entire flow of materials through the economy. By planning during the design and production stages for the dismantlement of motor vehicles, household appliances, and other sources of scrap, as some manufacturers are now doing, limitations on the reclamation of steel and other valuable substances can be lifted. Automobiles, for example, can be built without copper and other elements that hinder recycling, or processes can be designed in advance that allow for ease in the disassembly of products after disposal. That is where the fullest potential for recycling lies.

A mature industrial society with a stable population size could live largely on recycled steel, with air and water pollution only a small fraction of what they are when primary minerals are used. Except for losses due to impurities, rusting, and the unavoidable loss of some steel from recycling, metal can be used over and over again, indefinitely.

# Nuclear Waste Accumulating                    Nicholas Lenssen

Half a century after the world's nuclear industries began accumulating radioactive waste, not a single one of the more than 25 countries producing nuclear power has found a safe, permanent way to dispose of it. Nuclear waste remains dangerous for hundreds of thousands of years—meaning that in producing it, today's governments assume responsibility for the fate of thousands of future generations.

Despite the needed short-term focus on the radioactive waste at nuclear weapons facilities, it is civilian nuclear power that has produced roughly 95 percent of the radioactivity emanating from waste in the world. In 1990, the world's 424 commercial nuclear reactors created some 9,500 tons of irradiated fuel, bringing the total accumulation of used fuel to 84,000 tons—twice as much as in 1985.[1] (See Figure 1.) The United States houses a quarter of this, with a radioactivity of more than 20 billion curies.[2]

Since the beginning of the nuclear age, there has been no shortage of ideas on how to isolate radioactive waste from the biosphere. Scientists have proposed burying it under Antarctic ice, injecting it into the seabed, or hurling it into outer space. But each proposal brought an array of objections. As these have mounted, authorities have fallen back on the idea of burying radioactive waste hundreds of feet below the earth's crust.[3]

The concept of geologic burial is fairly straightforward. Engineers would begin by hollowing out a repository at least a quarter-mile below the earth's surface. This would consist of a broadly dispersed series of rooms from which thermally hot waste would be placed in holes drilled in the host rock. When the chamber is ready, waste would be transported to the burial site, where technicians would package it in specially constructed containers made of stainless steel or other metal.

Once placed in the rock, the containers would be surrounded by an impermeable material such as clay to retard groundwater penetration, then sealed with cement. When the repository is full, it would be sealed off from the surface.[4] Finally, workers would erect some everlasting signpost to the future, warning generations millennia hence of the deadly radioactivity entombed below.[5]

Geologic disposal, however, as with any human contrivance meant to last thousands of years, is little more than a calculated risk. Scientists still heatedly debate the possibility of disturbance of the waste by groundwater, geological activity, or human intervention. As Stanford University geologist Konrad Krauskopf wrote in *Science* in 1990, "No scientist or engineer can give an absolute guarantee that radioactive waste will not someday leak in dangerous quantities from even the best of repositories."[6]

According to a 1990 National Research Council report on radioactive waste disposal, predicting future conditions that could affect a burial site stretches the limits of human understanding in several areas of geology, groundwater movement, and chemistry. "Studies done over the past two decades have led to the realization that the phenomena are more complicated than had been thought," notes the report.[7]

Since the early days of nuclear power, scientists have issued warnings about the long-lived danger of radioactive waste. In 1957, a U.S. National Academy of Sciences panel cautioned that "unlike the disposal of any other type of waste, the hazard related to radioactive wastes is so great that no element of doubt should be allowed to exist regarding safety."[8] In 1960, another Academy committee urged that the waste issue be resolved before new nuclear facilities are licensed.[9]

Yet such recommendations fell on deaf ears, and one country after another plunged ahead with building nuclear power plants. As government bureaucrats and industry spokespeople promoted their new industry, they attempted to quiet any public uneasiness about waste storage with assurances that it could be dealt with. However, early failures of waste storage and burial practices engendered growing mistrust of the secretive government nuclear agencies that were responsible. For example, three of the six shallow burial sites for commercial low-level radioactive waste in the United States—in Kentucky, Illinois, and New York—have already leaked waste and been closed.[10] And the cost of cleaning up the Department of Energy's military sites could run to as much as $300 billion and still not be completed.[11]

Government officials frequently suggest that

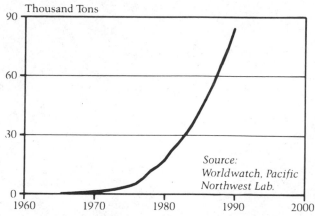

**Figure 1: Cumulative Generation of Irradiated Fuel from Commercial Nuclear Plants, 1965–90**

the waste issue has been solved in other countries. Yet no nation has developed a proven method of containing radioactive waste permanently. By their own timetables, in fact, most governments have found their efforts to bury waste moving in reverse. In France, large protests in 1989 and 1990 forced Prime Minister Michel Rocard to impose a nationwide moratorium on studying radioactive waste burial grounds.[12] The government launched a new attempt to explore sites in 1991, but no decision on a final burial place will be made for at least 15 years.[13]

In 1975, the United States planned on having a high-level waste burial site operating by 1985. The date was moved to 1989, then to 1998, 2003, and now 2010—a goal that still appears unrealistic, given technical questions and the vehement opposition of the state of Nevada. This has led former U.S. Nuclear Regulatory Commissioner Victor Gilinsky to describe the program as a "political dead-end."[14]

Germany expected in the mid-eighties to open its deep burial facility at the Gorleben salt dome by 1998, but the government waste agency now cites 2008 as the target year.[15] Public opposition and technical uncertainties have delayed work. Indeed, groundwater from neighboring sand and gravel layers is eroding the salt that makes up the Gorleben dome, and one worker was killed by collapsing rock during a 1987 drilling accident, further eroding public confidence.[16]

The Japanese government also has run into public opposition to its burial plans. In 1984, planners selected the village of Horonobe near the northern tip of Hokkaido Island.[17] But opposition from the Hokkaido Prefecture governor and legislature and from nearby villagers and farmers has blocked the government from constructing the waste storage and underground research facility.[18] There are signs that Japan is now looking beyond its borders for a solution. Since 1984, China has shown interest in importing irradiated fuel or waste for either a fee or in return for assistance with its own fledgling nuclear program.[19] In November 1990, China and Japan agreed to build an underground facility in China's Shanxi province, where research is to be undertaken on high-level waste burial.[20]

Above-ground "temporary" storage appears to be the de facto solution facing many nations, including the United States, well into the twenty-first century. Temporary storage—using improved storage methods—at least offers the best chance of buying time while the search for a technologically and socially feasible route continues. Addressing the waste problem also requires regaining public confidence in the responsible institutions.[21]

# Economic Features

# Arms Trade Exceeds Grain          Michael Renner

The international trade in both arms and grain has been on a roller coaster since the early seventies. The total amount of money spent on arms transactions trailed that expended on grain during the sixties. Arms exports moved ahead in 1972; the two trends seesawed during the seventies, and then arms moved ahead for good in 1980.[1] (See Figure 1.)

Arms exports were propelled upwards primarily by the large-scale purchases of sophisticated weaponry by Middle Eastern countries following the oil crises in 1973 and 1979-80. Military imports into the region surged almost fivefold, from about $5.5 billion in 1972 to a peak of $26.8 billion in 1984 (in 1990 dollars).[2]

Since then, however, international arms sales have dropped by almost 30 percent, from $66 billion to $47 billion.[3] The Third World debt crisis made the acquisition of weapons much less affordable for a large number of countries. Even many of the oil-exporting countries, after an unprecedented spending spree, had to adjust to leaner times as petroleum prices collapsed. Only the 1980-88 Iran-Iraq war and expanded purchases by India cushioned this rapid fall in arms sales.

With the end of the cold war, the weapons industries of the United States and the former Soviet Union—by far the dominant arms peddlers—are set to shrink. According to the Stockholm International Peace Research Institute (SIPRI), U.S. exports of major weapons systems declined by a quarter from 1989 to 1990, but Soviet sales fell by almost 50 percent.[4] In February 1992, Russian President Yeltsin called continued arms exports an ''unavoidable necessity,'' but they are clearly no solution to the huge overcapacities in the arms industry of the Commonwealth of Independent States.[5]

Meanwhile, in the grain market, rising demand combined with even more rapidly rising prices pushed the value of global trade to record levels in the early seventies. At a period of already tightening global supplies, the 1972 Soviet decision to import large quantities of wheat to offset its harvest shortfalls triggered the jump in prices. The volume of grain imports continued to in-

crease until 1980, but prices worked their way back down. Expressed in constant dollars, they soon returned to the levels prevalent in the sixties. During the first half of the eighties, the continued erosion of grain prices coincided with a gradual decline in the volume of grain sales, producing a steep fall in the overall value of grain trade.[6]

It is tempting to contrast arms and grain trade by regarding one as objectionable and the other as desirable. Although arms merchants will claim that their wares are intended only for defensive purposes, weapons are undoubtedly the bearers

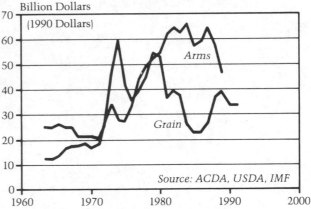

**Figure 1: World Arms and Grain Trade, 1963–91**

of death and destruction. And since they add nothing to a nation's consumption or its productive capacity, arms waste precious resources. But growing agricultural trade is not necessarily a blessing either. Rising grain imports are often a testament to a country's inability to feed itself, implying a dangerous reliance on foreign supplies. Indeed, food has repeatedly been used as a political weapon.

One interesting parallel between the trade in arms and grain is the remarkably small number of countries supplying the world. Only six countries—primarily the former Soviet Union and the United States, followed by France, Britain, Germany, and China—account for close to 90 percent of the global arms bazaar.[7] The global grain trade is dominated by the United States, which was responsible for nearly 60 percent of all net exports in 1988. Canada and the European Community each accounted for 15 percent or so, followed by Australia, with 8 percent.[8]

It now appears that the elevated arms trade in the seventies and eighties was a short-term situation, not a long-term trend. SIPRI observed in its 1988 *Yearbook* that "the depression of the Third World arms trade in the eighties can no longer be dismissed as a temporary aberration. These countries are not buying major weapons as avidly as they did in the late seventies." The group concluded that "the scarcity of new orders suggests that future deliveries will decline."[9]

Instead of buying new equipment, many governments are increasingly turning to retrofitting and modernizing existing hardware. SIPRI further explains that "other forms of transfer—licensed production [in the recipient country], technology transfer, retrofit and modernization, small transactions, and the grey and black markets—often rival the significance of the orthodox sales of major weapons."[10]

The conclusion of the Iran-Iraq war in 1988 meant that suppliers were hard-pressed to find customers as voracious in their appetites for deadly equipment as the two Gulf states. In addition, since its invasion of Kuwait, Iraq—one of the world's leading arms importers—has been under an international embargo. Saudi Arabia, on the other hand, already a major buyer of military hardware, continues large-scale purchases in the wake of a conflict that suddenly transformed it into a frontline state.

The demand for arms in other hot spots may shrink to the degree that war weariness drives combatants to embrace the United Nations as a peacemaker and that U.N. mediation proves successful in settling conflicts. China, for example, claims to have stopped arms supplies to its allies in Kampuchea in 1990.[11] Even as Soviet forces withdrew from Afghanistan, arms flows into that country surged as a bitter civil war continued to rage. Following a 1991 U.S.-Soviet agreement to stop arms deliveries, however, these flows likely declined dramatically. Pakistan, a major conduit for weapons to the Afghan *mujahedeen*, joined the embargo.

The global grain trade, on the other hand, is likely to expand over the long term. During 1988, the drought in various regions of the world sent grain prices up for the first time in a decade, although the amount traded has not changed much. With global grain reserves at one of the lowest levels in many years, a severe drought in any major grain-growing region could send prices climbing.

Thus, in all likelihood the global trade in grains may soon exceed that in arms for the first time since the mid-seventies. A good deal of that will be due to a lessening in conflicts as well as the inability of some countries to afford new weapons. Unfortunately, the other reason may be that growing grain deficits in Africa, Asia, and the Commonwealth of Independent States could push the dollar value of grain trade to record levels.

# Wheat/Oil Exchange Rate Shifts       Lester R. Brown

The economic fortunes of nations rise and fall with shifts in the exchange rate between two widely traded commodities: grain and oil. Grain, which supplies half of human caloric intake when consumed directly and a sizable share of the remainder in the form of livestock products, dominates the world food economy.[1] Likewise, oil—a highly versatile fuel that accounts for some 40 percent of commercial energy use—rules the world energy economy.[2]

Exports of each commodity are concentrated in a handful of countries, with grain coming largely from North America and oil from the Middle East. The United States, which dominates grain exports even more than Saudi Arabia does oil, is both the world's leading grain exporter and its biggest oil importer.[3] And, ironically, all 13 members of the Organization of Petroleum Exporting Countries (OPEC) are grain importers.[4]

Although the trade balances in importers of oil or grain are influenced by price changes, the countries that depend heavily on exports of one to pay for imports of the other are most dramatically affected by shifts in the grain/oil exchange rate. Using the price of wheat as a surrogate for grain prices, shifts in that exchange rate can be easily monitored.

From 1950 through 1972, the prices of both wheat and oil exhibited an extraordinary degree of stability. So too, therefore, did the exchange rate between the two. When OPEC tripled oil prices at the end of 1973, it created an instability that has prevailed ever since. In 1950, when wheat was priced at $1.89 a bushel and oil at $1.71 a barrel, a bushel of wheat could be exchanged for 1.1 barrels of oil. (See Table 1.) In 1972, just one year before the first oil price hike, a bushel of wheat and a barrel of oil were both worth exactly $1.90. At any time during this 22-year span, a bushel of wheat could be exchanged for a barrel of oil on the world market.

By 1979, the year of the second oil price increase, OPEC's strength had pushed the exchange rate to roughly four to one. This steep rise in the purchasing power of oil led to one of the greatest international transfers of wealth ever recorded. The coffers of major oil exporters such as Saudi Arabia began to overflow with dollars as those of many oil-importing countries were being emptied.

By 1982, wheat prices had weakened slightly and the price of oil had edged above $33 a barrel, requiring a record eight bushels of wheat to buy a barrel of oil. Within 10 years, the terms of trade for oil-exporting countries that import wheat had improved eightfold. For countries that export grain to pay for oil, such as the United States, it was an impoverishing shift.

During the eighties, the cumulative effect of expanded non-OPEC production and successful energy conservation programs in the major industrial countries began to undermine OPEC efforts to sustain high oil prices. Oil prices fell by nearly half between 1985 and 1986, to less than $14 a barrel, reducing the exchange rate to six to one in 1987.

In 1991, heat and drought sharply reduced grain harvests in both the United States and the Soviet Union, the world's second- and third-ranking producers.[5] As a result, wheat prices strengthened in late 1991 and even more in early 1992, rising well above $4 per bushel. Meanwhile, oil prices, which had climbed sharply in late 1990 and early 1991 with supply disruptions during the Gulf War, began to moderate in late 1991 and early 1992. The result was a moderate decline in the wheat-oil exchange rate from six in 1990 to five in 1991.

The dramatic, historical shift in the wheat-oil exchange rate that started in 1974 altered the economic fortunes of many countries, but perhaps none more than the United States. During the early seventies, U.S. grain exports easily paid the nation's oil import bill. But the nation's failure to wean itself from heavy dependence on this increasingly costly commodity contributed to soaring outlays for imports, the emergence of a trade deficit, and mounting external debt. In contrast, such oil-exporting/grain-importing countries as Saudi Arabia, Iran, Iraq, Algeria, and Libya benefitted handsomely.

No one can project exactly when the wheat/oil exchange rate will shift again, or even in which direction it will go, but a long-term change in favor of grain exporters seems unlikely. Knowing this, countries that export grain and import oil can invest in auto fuel efficiency, alternatives to

TABLE 1: THE WHEAT-OIL EXCHANGE
RATE, 1950–91

| YEAR | BUSHEL OF WHEAT (dollars) | BARREL OF OIL (dollars) | BUSHELS OF WHEAT TO BUY ONE BARREL OF OIL |
|---|---|---|---|
| 1950 | 1.89 | 1.71 | 1 |
| 1951 | 2.03 | 1.71 | 1 |
| 1952 | 1.93 | 1.71 | 1 |
| 1953 | 1.89 | 1.93 | 1 |
| 1954 | 1.98 | 1.93 | 1 |
| 1955 | 1.81 | 1.93 | 1 |
| 1956 | 1.84 | 1.93 | 1 |
| 1957 | 1.79 | 2.02 | 1 |
| 1958 | 1.62 | 2.08 | 1 |
| 1959 | 1.58 | 1.92 | 1 |
| 1960 | 1.58 | 1.50 | 1 |
| 1961 | 1.60 | 1.45 | 1 |
| 1962 | 1.75 | 1.42 | 1 |
| 1963 | 1.76 | 1.40 | 1 |
| 1964 | 1.84 | 1.33 | 1 |
| 1965 | 1.62 | 1.33 | 1 |
| 1966 | 1.71 | 1.33 | 1 |
| 1967 | 1.79 | 1.33 | 1 |
| 1968 | 1.71 | 1.30 | 1 |
| 1969 | 1.59 | 1.28 | 1 |
| 1970 | 1.49 | 1.30 | 1 |
| 1971 | 1.68 | 1.65 | 1 |
| 1972 | 1.90 | 1.90 | 1 |
| 1973 | 3.81 | 2.70 | 1 |
| 1974 | 4.89 | 9.76 | 2 |
| 1975 | 4.06 | 10.72 | 3 |
| 1976 | 3.62 | 11.51 | 3 |
| 1977 | 2.81 | 12.40 | 4 |
| 1978 | 3.48 | 12.70 | 4 |
| 1979 | 4.36 | 17.26 | 4 |
| 1980 | 4.70 | 28.67 | 6 |
| 1981 | 4.76 | 32.50 | 7 |
| 1982 | 4.36 | 33.47 | 8 |
| 1983 | 4.28 | 29.31 | 7 |
| 1984 | 4.15 | 28.25 | 7 |
| 1985 | 3.70 | 26.98 | 7 |
| 1986 | 3.13 | 13.82 | 4 |
| 1987 | 3.07 | 17.79 | 6 |
| 1988 | 3.95 | 14.15 | 4 |
| 1989 | 4.61 | 17.19 | 4 |
| 1990 | 3.69 | 22.05 | 6 |
| 1991 (est) | 3.40 | 18.50 | 5 |

the automobile, and alternative fuels. For the United States, adoption of auto fuel-efficiency standards and a stiff gasoline tax approaching those in Europe and Japan would help minimize the effect of any future decline in the wheat-oil exchange rate by reducing U.S. dependence on imported oil. This in turn would reduce the on-going heavy outflow of U.S. dollars.

SOURCES: International Monetary Fund, *International Financial Statistics,* various years.

# Social
## Features

# Income Distribution Worsening
## Alan Thein Durning

Since 1900, the value of goods and services produced each year worldwide has grown twentyfold, the use of energy thirtyfold, the products of industry fiftyfold, and the average distance traveled by the well-to-do perhaps a thousandfold.[1] But that expansion has not been distributed equally among people.

In the nineties, the standard of living of the world's affluent nations is unprecedented. Nonetheless, the gap between rich and poor is widening. The world has 202 billionaires and perhaps 3 million millionaires, but 100 million people around the globe are homeless, living on sidewalks, in garbage dumps, and under bridges.[2]

Americans spend $5 billion each year on special diets to lower their calorie consumption, while the world's poorest 400 million people are so undernourished that they are likely to suffer stunted growth, mental retardation, or death.[3] As water from a single spring in France is bottled and shipped to the prosperous around the world, 1.9 billion people drink and bathe in water contaminated with parasites and bacteria, and more than half of humanity lacks sanitary toilets.[4] In 1988, the world's nation-states devoted $1 trillion—$200 for each person on the planet—to the means of warfare, but failed to scrape together the $5 per child it would have cost to eradicate the simple diseases that killed 14 million children that year.[5]

Destitution in the modern world is perpetuated by a set of mutually reinforcing factors that form a global poverty trap. Locally, poor people's lack of productive assets and their physical weakness, susceptibility to illness, and powerlessness combine with rapid population growth to keep them in constrained circumstances. Nationally, government policies in many sectors favor the urban fortunate over the rural masses. And at the international level, interlocking patterns of debt, trade, and capital flight during the eighties have made the rich richer and the poor poorer.

In recent times, moreover, poverty has become an increasingly environmental phenomenon. The poor not only suffer disproportionately from environmental damage caused by the better off, they have become a major cause of ecological decline themselves. Pushed to marginal lands by population growth and inequitable development patterns, they raze plots in the rain forest, plow steep slopes, and overgraze fragile rangeland. Economic deprivation and environmental degradation have thus come to reinforce one another to form a downward spiral that threatens to pull ever more into its grasp.

In 1978, Robert McNamara, then president of the World Bank, gave what stands as the classic description of absolute poverty: "A condition of life so limited by malnutrition, illiteracy, disease, squalid surroundings, high infant mortality, and low life expectancy as to be beneath any reasonable definition of human decency."[6] As McNamara's words suggest, poverty is far more than an economic condition.

Although traditionally measured in terms of income, poverty's true horror, as revealed by what poor people strive most persistently to escape, extends into all aspects of individual life: susceptibility to disease, lack of access to most types of services and information, lack of control over resources, subordination to higher social and economic classes, vulnerability to sudden misfortunes, and insecurity in the face of changing circumstances. Flowing from these physical dimensions, poverty's psychological toll is equally severe—the erosion of human dignity and self-respect.

The World Bank says that more than 1 billion people in the developing world today live in poverty.[7] During the eighties, per capita incomes declined dramatically in sub-Saharan Africa and slightly in Latin America, as well as in parts of Asia, swamping improvements in other areas like China and India. Without direct monitoring, however, tracking the course of poverty requires inference from trends in average incomes, wages, prices, unemployment rates, and other indicators.[8]

Based on income data adjusted for regional differences in purchasing power by Robert Summers and Alan Heston of the University of Pennsylvania, some 60 percent of the world's people live in countries where annual income per person is below $2,000. Of the 5 percent of the world's people with the highest incomes, most live in the United States.[9]

And within countries, the gap between rich people and poor is larger than average incomes would suggest: between 60 and 70 percent of the people in most countries earn less than their nation's average income. Almost nowhere does the poorest fifth of households collect 10 percent of national income, while the richest fifth commonly receives half.[10] (See Table 1.)

Among the world's most populous nations, China, the former Soviet Union, and Japan all have relatively equitable income distributions, with the richest fifth of households in the nation receiving between three and four times as much per year as the poorest fifth. Indonesia, Egypt, and India fall in the middle of the range, with the rich earning 8-10 times as much as the poor. Mexico is less even, with a factor of 18 separating top and bottom, while in Brazil members of the richest fifth earn 28 times as much as members of the poorest fifth.

Income measurements, however, are not always a good indicator of how well off people are. In 1985, for example, Egypt's per capita income was about half of Peru's, but because Egypt is more equitable, poor Egyptians earned one third more than poor Peruvians. Likewise, Brazil's average income was twice Sri Lanka's, but the Sri Lankan poor earned more than the Brazilian poor.[11]

Worldwide, the fifth of humanity living in the richest countries have average incomes 15 times higher than the fifth living in the poorest. If all the world's 5.5 billion people were individually ranked according to income and the income of the richest one fifth were compared to that of the poorest one fifth, it would show a much wider gap. Economists Ronald Sprout and James Weaver, who have attempted to do this, conclude that after adjusting income for purchasing power, the ratio between the richest and poorest one fifths of humanity is at least 30 to 1.[12]

Adapted from *Poverty and the Environment: Reversing the Downward Spiral*, Worldwatch Paper 92

TABLE 1: APPROXIMATE INCOME DISTRIBUTION OF MOST POPULOUS NATIONS, AND OF WORLD, MOST RECENT AVAILABLE YEAR[1]

| COUNTRY | YEAR | SHARE OF NATIONAL INCOME POOREST 20 PERCENT OF HOUSEHOLDS | SHARE OF NATIONAL INCOME RICHEST 20 PERCENT OF HOUSEHOLDS | RATIO OF RICHEST SHARE TO POOREST |
|---|---|---|---|---|
| China (cities) | 1984 | 12 | 31 | 3 |
| Soviet Union | 1980 | 9 | 36 | 4 |
| Japan | 1979 | 9 | 37 | 4 |
| W. Germany | 1978 | 8 | 40 | 5 |
| Unit. Kingdom | 1982 | 7 | 40 | 6 |
| Italy | 1977 | 6 | 44 | 7 |
| Indonesia | 1976 | 7 | 49 | 8 |
| Egypt | 1974 | 6 | 48 | 8 |
| India | 1976 | 5 | 50 | 10 |
| Philippines | 1985 | 5 | 53 | 10 |
| United States | 1986 | 4 | 46 | 12 |
| France | 1975 | 4 | 50 | 13 |
| Turkey | 1973 | 4 | 57 | 16 |
| Mexico | 1977 | 3 | 54 | 18 |
| Brazil | 1982 | 2 | 64 | 28 |
| World[2] | 1985 | 4 | 58 | 15 |

[1]Equity ratios are based on unrounded income share figures and therefore may appear inconsistent with income shares listed. [2]Estimated from average national incomes; income distribution based on individual incomes is much less equitable. SOURCE: Worldwatch Institute, based on various sources.

# Maternal Mortality Takes Heavy Toll     Jodi L. Jacobson

The World Health Organization defines maternal mortality as a death during or within 42 days of a pregnancy from causes related to or aggravated by the pregnancy or its management.[1] At least 500,000 women die annually from pregnancy-related causes. Ninety-nine percent of them live in developing countries.[2]

Complications of pregnancy, childbirth, and unsafe abortion are thus the leading killers of women of reproductive age throughout the Third World. From 20 to 45 percent of all deaths among women aged 15-49 are from pregnancy-related causes in most developing countries, compared with less than 1 percent in the United States and most of Europe.[3]

In terms of health indicators, there is no more telling measure of the gap between rich and poor countries than the rate of maternal death. The risk of maternal death is often more than 100 times as great in the Third World as in industrial countries. Conservative projections indicate illness and death from reproductive causes will continue rising: more than 600,000 women are expected to die each year from complications of pregnancy and unsafe abortion by decade's end, 20 percent more than the number of such deaths in 1992.[4]

Repeated childbearing under unsafe circumstances increases the lifetime risk of dying in pregnancy in the Third World. In Africa, for example, women face a 1 in 21 chance of dying from pregnancy-related causes in their lifetimes. (See Table 1.) In contrast, the odds in the United States are 1 in 6,366.[5]

Women in the Third World have all the major risk factors for poor maternal health, including illiteracy, poverty, and poor nutrition; 20 years or more of childbearing each; and inadequate or nonexistent health care. Each of these conditions multiplies severalfold the health risks women face throughout their lifetimes.

In absolute terms, South Asia has both the largest number of women of reproductive age and the highest number of maternal deaths annually—about 300,000. Bangladesh, Bhutan, India, Nepal, Pakistan, and Sri Lanka account for fully 43 percent of all maternal deaths. Africa is second in total mortality, with an estimated 150,000 pregnancy-related deaths each year, followed by Latin America with 34,000.[6]

For every woman who dies, many others are left with illnesses or impairments that rob them of their health and productivity, often for the rest of their lives. Pregnancy-related morbidity, or illness, is not well documented at the global level, but available studies suggest the toll is high. In India, for example, a village survey found 16 pregnancy-related illnesses for every maternal death. Extrapolating from this, World Bank researchers calculate that 3-12 percent of all pregnancies worldwide result in serious illness among women.[7]

In the majority of countries with data, hemorrhage and complications of unsafe abortion are the two most important causes of maternal death.[8] High rates of preexisting anemia and the general scarcity of blood for transfusions in developing countries are major contributing factors to deaths from hemorrhage. Complications of unsafe abortion, already the leading cause of death among women of reproductive age in Latin America, appear to be increasing in significance throughout Africa and Asia.[9]

Unsafe abortion and hemorrhage together account for more than 30 percent of maternal deaths in Ethiopia, India, Tanzania, and Zambia. Unsafe abortion alone is responsible for 31 percent of recorded maternal deaths in Bangladesh, hemorrhage for 22 percent, and toxemia for 19 percent. In the United States, where safe abor-

TABLE 1. LIFETIME RISK OF DYING FROM PREGNANCY-RELATED CAUSES, BY REGION, 1987

| REGION | RISK |
| --- | --- |
| Africa | 1 in 21 |
| Asia | 1 in 54 |
| Latin America | 1 in 73 |
| United States | 1 in 6,366 |
| Northern Europe | 1 in 9,850 |

SOURCE: Ann Starrs, *Preventing the Tragedy of Maternal Deaths: A Report on the International Safe Motherhood Conference* (Nairobi, Kenya: 1987).

tion services are still far more widely available than in developing countries, complications of abortion are next-to-last in importance as a cause of maternal deaths.[10]

Although a given death can always be traced back to a medical condition, the real "causes" of poor maternal health are rooted deeply in the social, cultural, and economic barriers faced by females in the Third World throughout their lifetimes. Malnutrition, for example, is far more prevalent among females there for reasons that have more to do with gender than geography. Discrimination against women in the allocation of food—as well as health care and education—is a widespread and well-documented practice in much of South Asia, for example, where strong preferences for male children diminish the "value" of females.[11]

About 60 percent of pregnant women and 47 percent of nonpregnant women in developing countries outside China are estimated to suffer from anemia. The prevalence of this condition is highest in South Asia and Africa. Anemia may increase the risk of dying in childbirth by a factor of four; severe anemia is associated with an eightfold risk of maternal death during pregnancy.[12]

Malnutrition often grows more acute over the course of a woman's life as a result of the combined effects of an increasingly heavy workload, the loss of iron stores through menstruation, and the physical demands of childbearing. These nutritional deficits contribute to what may become lifelong handicaps, such as an increased predisposition to illness, low weight, and stunted physical and mental development. Physical immaturity due to stunted growth subsequently leads to far higher rates of pregnancy-related problems,

including obstructed labor, cervical trauma, toxemia, ruptured uterus, infection, and hemorrhage. Under these conditions, women are ill-prepared for childbearing.

Lack of access to timely and effective basic maternal health care is a critical problem for Third World women. Prenatal care is instrumental in reducing complications associated with toxemia, obstructed labor, and infection, in providing preventive education to women on subjects such as nutrition during pregnancy, and in encouraging women to use a trained birth attendant. A study in Indonesia found that women who received no prenatal care were more than five times as likely to die from pregnancy-related causes as those who attended a prenatal clinic.[13]

Throughout South Asia and much of Africa, however, only 20-35 percent of women receive adequate prenatal care. Most women face the prospect of giving birth without trained medical assistance. Only about a third of all births are assisted by trained attendants in Africa and South Asia, as opposed to 64 percent in Latin America, 93 percent in East Asia, and virtually 100 percent in North America.[14]

In many Third World communities, traditional birth attendants—usually village-based women untrained in modern medicine—are the only source of maternal health care or the only affordable alternative to clinics. Like those they serve, these women are usually poor, illiterate, and guided by sometimes-harmful traditional practices. Because relatively few countries have put resources into training traditional attendants, their potential for reducing illness and deaths related to pregnancy remains largely untapped.[15]

# Coerced Motherhood Increasing     Jodi L. Jacobson

Pregnancy and childbirth cannot be considered voluntary unless a woman can answer the following questions affirmatively: Can I control when and with whom I have sexual relations? Can I choose when and how to regulate my fertility, free from dangerous or undesirable side-effects of contraception? Can I obtain a safe abortion on request? For the vast majority of women worldwide, the answer to one or all of these questions is a resounding "no."

Since the mid-eighties, the number of women who can exercise the right to decide freely on the number and spacing of their children has been declining, leading to a global increase in coerced pregnancy and motherhood. These basic human rights are under siege in virtually every country. Women in the United States, Germany, and Poland, for example, face increasing hurdles to preventing or terminating unwanted pregnancies.[1] And coerced pregnancy and childbirth long have been commonplace in the many developing nations where the majority of women lack access to contraception or safe abortion services.

Limits on access to family planning methods, including abortion, directly contradict international agreements. In 1968, the member states of the United Nations unanimously recognized the human right to decide freely on the number and spacing of children.[2] Ten years later, the United Nations confirmed the universal right to reproductive health care, including family planning, maternal health, and the prevention and treatment of common sexually transmitted diseases (STDs).[3]

Death and illness result often from such coercion. This year at least 1 million women will die of reproductive causes—including complications of childbirth, unsafe abortion, and sexually transmitted diseases—while more than 100 million others will suffer disabling illnesses.[4]

For one thing, fertility is so highly valued in many cultures that women come under enormous pressure to marry and bear their first child as soon as possible. Indeed, in parts of South Asia and sub-Saharan Africa, a childless woman is subject to abandonment, abuse, or even murder.[5] As a result, women may share little bargaining power in the bedroom. Sexual coercion, ranging from marital rape to more subtle forms of pressure, is a problem for women everywhere, but is particularly acute in countries where women are disproportionately poor, poorly educated, and politically powerless.

TABLE 1: ABORTION LAWS WORLDWIDE, BY NUMBER OF COUNTRIES AND SHARE OF WORLD POPULATION

| LEGAL CONDITIONS | COUNTRIES[1] (number) | SHARE OF WORLD POPULATION (percent) |
|---|---|---|
| Life endangerment[2] | 53 | 25 |
| Other maternal health reasons | 42 | 12 |
| Social and sociomedical reasons | 14 | 23 |
| No mandated conditions[3] | 23 | 40 |

[1]Countries with populations of at least 1 million. [2]Technically, in some countries in this category abortion is prohibited without exception. [3]Includes some of the world's most populous countries (China, the former Soviet Union, and the United States).
SOURCE: Stanley K. Hensaw, "Induced Abortion: A World Review, 1990," *Family Planning Perspectives,* March/April 1990.

Studies in Africa have shown that women's economic impoverishment leaves them vulnerable to both unwanted pregnancy and STDs. The African man maintains "unrestrained and unchallenged dominance over the African woman," according to E. Maxine Ankrah, a lecturer at Makerere University in Kampala, Uganda. Her survey of 144 Ugandan women found that women faced an almost total "lack of decision-making power in matters of sex," and they stated that in matters of family planning their husbands "won't cooperate."[6]

Women in Mexico face similar problems. As many as 60 percent of those who seek state-sponsored birth control must do so without the knowledge of their husbands, in large part because of the prevailing belief among men that contraceptive use will diminish their manhood or lead to infidelity. A wife found surreptitiously practicing birth control risks physical abuse.[7] Under these constraints, a woman's ability to negotiate protective measures is clearly minimal.

Aside from social pressures, as many as 300 million married women of reproductive age worldwide would like to prevent pregnancies but have no access to reliable birth control, according to the U.N. Population Fund.[8] More than half of all pregnancies among U.S. women each year are unintended, partly because many women cannot afford contraception.[9]

Socially and ethically, abortion is generally recognized as a method of last resort, although in terms of health it is one of the safest available methods of fertility control. Relatively few women have access to safe abortion services even in countries where abortion is in theory legal. (See Table 1.) Last year in Kenya, 71 female students were raped and 17 died in a mass attack by male students.[10] Under Kenyan law, any resulting pregnancy would have to be carried to term. Moreover, laws and policies in parts of Africa, Latin America, and Muslim Asia effectively prohibit abortion even to save a woman's life.[11]

Demographers have calculated that in the absence of contraception, a woman wanting only two children would require an average of 9-10 abortions in her lifetime.[12] Indeed, in the former Soviet Union, where contraceptives remain scarce, women average 7-10 abortions.[13]

Contraceptives reduce but do not eliminate the need for access to abortion. They can fail: 7 out of 10 women using a 95-percent effective method of birth control, such as the pill, would still require at least one abortion in their lifetime to achieve a two-child family.[14]

Moreover, the methods of birth control most effective in preventing the spread of AIDS and other sexually transmitted diseases, namely the condom and diaphragm, are generally less effective in preventing conception. Women choosing these methods to protect themselves from both unwanted pregnancy and STDs will invariably face a greater need for access to abortion to terminate an unwanted pregnancy, a connection that most public health initiatives do not acknowledge.

The same societies that hold women hostage to pregnancy by denying them access to contraception and safe abortion are the most apt to punish them if they do become pregnant out of wedlock. For many, the social consequences of unwed motherhood—which often include ostracism or violent abuse by family members—outweigh the potential dangers of unsafe abortion. A study in Bangladesh, for example, found that unmarried women aged 15-19 were 10 times more likely to die from abortion than their married peers. Many choose to take their own lives: nearly three fourths of all maternal deaths among unmarried women in Bangladesh were related to either suicide or unsafe abortion.[15]

# NOTES

## GRAIN HARVEST DROPS

1. U.S. Department of Agriculture (USDA), *World Grain Situation and Outlook*, Washington, D.C., March 1992 and earlier editions.
2. USDA, *World Grain Situation and Outlook*, Washington, D.C., December 1991 and earlier editions.
3. USDA, *World Agricultural Production*, Washington, D.C., March 1992.
4. USDA, *World Grain Situation and Outlook*, various issues.
5. USDA, *World Grain Situation and Outlook*, Washington, D.C., September 1991.
6. Yuri Markish, "Inputs in Soviet Agriculture," *Centrally Planned Economies Agriculture Report*, USDA, Washington, D.C., July/August 1991; USDA, *USSR Agriculture and Trade Report*, Washington, D.C., May 1991.
7. USDA, *World Grain Situation and Outlook*, March 1992.
8. USDA, *Agricultural Resources*, Washington, D.C., September 1991; USDA, *World Grain Situation and Outlook*, March 1992.
9. U.N. Food and Agriculture Organization (FAO), *Production Yearbook 1990* (Rome: 1990); Bill Quimby, Economic Research Service, USDA, Washington, D.C., private communication, March 20, 1992.
10. FAO, *Fertilizer Yearbook* (Rome: various years); The Fertilizer Institute, *Fertilizer Facts and Figures, 1990* (Washington, D.C.: 1990); USDA, Economic Research Service, *World Grain Database* (unpublished printouts) (Washington, D.C.: 1991).
11. For a more detailed discussion of the effects of environmental degradation on food production, see Lester R. Brown and John Young, "Feeding the World in the Nineties," in Lester R. Brown et al., *State of the World 1990* (New York: W.W. Norton & Co., 1990).

## SOYBEAN PRODUCTION UP

1. U.S. Department of Agriculture (USDA), *World Oilseed Situation and Outlook*, Washington, D.C., March 1992.
2. USDA, *World Oilseed Situation and Outlook*, Washington, D.C., various years.
3. U.S. Department of Commerce, Bureau of the Census, *Statistical Abstract of the United States: 1990* (Washington, D.C.: U.S. Government Printing Office, 1990).
4. Ibid.
5. USDA, *World Oilseed Situation and Outlook*, March 1992.
6. USDA, *World Oilseed Situation and Outlook*, various years.
7. USDA, *World Soybean Database* (unpublished printout) (Washington, D.C.: 1991).

## MEAT PRODUCTION RISES

1. U.N. Food and Agriculture Organization (FAO), *1948-1985 World Crop and Livestock Statistics* (Rome: 1987); FAO, *FAO Production Yearbooks* (Rome: various years); U.S. Department of Agriculture (USDA), *World Agricultural Production*, Washington, D.C., March 1992.
2. FAO, *1948-1985 World Crop and Livestock Statistics*; FAO, *FAO Production Yearbooks*; USDA, *World Agricultural Production*; World Bank Department of Socio-Economic Data, Washington, D.C., unpublished printout, February 1992.
3. United Nations, *World Population Prospects 1991* (New York: 1992).
4. FAO, *1948-1985 World Crop and Livestock Statistics*; FAO, *FAO Production Yearbooks*; USDA, *World Agricultural Production*; United Nations, *World Population Prospects 1991*.

5. U.S. Department of Interior, Bureau of Land Management, *Public Land Statistics 1987* (Washington, D.C.: 1988).

6. Southern African Development Coordination Conference, *Agriculture: Toward 2000* (Rome: FAO, 1984).

7. USDA, *World Grain Situation and Outlook*, Washington, D.C., December 1991; USDA, *World Population by Country and Region, 1990* (Washington, D.C.: 1990).

8. USDA, *World Oilseed Situation and Outlook*, Washington, D.C., May 1991.

9. Feed to poultry conversion ratio derived from data in Robert V. Bishop et al., *The World Poultry Market—Government Intervention and Multilaterial Policy Reform*, Staff Report #AGES 9019 (Washington, D.C.: USDA, 1990); conversion ratio for grain to beef based on Allen Baker, Feed Situation and Outlook staff, Economic Research Service (ERS), USDA, private communication, April 27, 1992, on Linda Bailey, Livestock and Poultry Situation staff, ERS, USDA, private communication, April 27, 1992, and on data taken from various issues of *Feedstuffs*; pork data from Leland Southard, Livestock and Poultry Situation and Outlook staff, ERS, USDA, private communication, April 27, 1992.

10. FAO, *1948-1985 World Crop and Livestock Statistics*; FAO, *FAO Production Yearbooks*; USDA, *World Agricultural Production*; World Bank, unpublished printout.

11. FAO, *1948-1985 World Crop and Livestock Statistics*; FAO, *FAO Production Yearbooks*; USDA, *World Agricultural Production*; World Bank, unpublished printout.

12. FAO, *1948-1985 World Crop and Livestock Statistics*; FAO, *FAO Production Yearbooks*; USDA, *World Agricultural Production*; World Bank, unpublished printout.

13. Lester R. Brown, "A Generation of Deficits," in Lester R. Brown et al., *State of the World 1986* (New York: W.W. Norton & Co., 1986).

14. FAO, *1948-1985 World Crop and Livestock Statistics*; FAO, *FAO Production Yearbooks*; USDA, *World Agricultural Production*; World Bank, unpublished printout.

15. Alan B. Durning and Holly B. Brough, *Taking Stock: Animal Farming and the Environment*, Worldwatch Paper 103 (Washington, D.C.: Worldwatch Institute, July 1991), citing USDA, Foreign Agricultural Service, "World Livestock Situation," April 1991, and Linda Bailey, agricultural economist, USDA, Washington, D.C., private communication, September 11, 1990.

## FISH CATCH FALLS

1. U.N. Food and Agriculture Organization (FAO), *FAO Yearbook: Fisheries Statistics, Commodities* (Rome: various years); 1990 data from FAO, Rome, private communication, February 1992.

2. World Resources Institute, *World Resources 1988-89* (New York: Basic Books, 1988).

3. FAO, *FAO Yearbook*; FAO, private communication.

4. World Resources Institute, *World Resources 1990-91* (New York: Oxford University Press, 1990).

5. U.N. Environment Programme (UNEP), *Environmental Data Report 1991-92* (Oxford: Basil Blackwell, 1991).

6. Nick Lenssen, "The Ocean Blues," *World Watch*, July/August 1989.

7. UNEP, *Environmental Data Report 1991-92*.

8. FAO, *Fish for Food and Development* (Rome: 1991).

9. Elmer A. Keen, *Ownership and Productivity of Marine Fishery Resources* (Blacksburg, Va.: McDonald and Woodward, 1988), cited in Lenssen, "The Ocean Blues."

10. Government of Newfoundland and Labrador, "Why Canada Must Act to Protect the Grand Banks Fishery," St. John's, Newfoundland, March 17, 1992.

11. FAO, *FAO Yearbook*; FAO, private communication.

## GRAIN STOCKS DECLINE

1. U.S. Department of Agriculture (USDA), *World Grain Situation and Outlook*, Washington, D.C., April 1992.

2. Ibid.

3. Ibid.; International Monetary Fund, *International Financial Statistics, 1991 Yearbook* (Washington, D.C.: 1991).

4. John Battersby, "Severe Drought Threatens Reform in Southern Africa," *Christian Science Monitor*, March 23, 1992.

5. USDA, Economic Research Service, *Agricultural Resources: Cropland, Water and Conservation Situation and Outlook Report*, Washington, D.C., September 1991.

6. USDA, *Agricultural Resources: Cropland, Water, and Conservation Situation and Outlook Report*, Washington, D.C., September 1991.

7. Worldwatch Institute calculation based on Alan B. Durning and Holly B. Brough, *Taking Stock: Animal Farming and the Environment*, Worldwatch Paper 103 (Washington, D.C.: Worldwatch Institute, July 1991).

## GRAINLAND SHRINKS

1. U.S. Department of Agriculture (USDA), *World Grain Situation and Outlook*, Washington, D.C., April 1992.
2. Ibid.
3. USDA, Economic Research Service (ERS), *World Grain Database* (unpublished printouts) (Washington, D.C.: 1991).
4. Ibid.
5. Ibid.
6. Ibid.
7. USDA, ERS, *China: Situation and Outlook Report*, Washington, D.C., July 1986.
8. United Nations, *World Economic Survey 1991* (New York: 1991).
9. USDA, ERS, *World Grain Database*.
10. David E. Dowall, "The Land Market Assessment: A New Tool for Urban Management," paper prepared for the Urban Management Program of United Nations Center for Human Settlements, World Bank, and United Nations Development Programme, University of California, Berkeley, March 1991.
11. Population Reference Bureau, *World Population Data Sheet 1991* (Washington, D.C.: 1991).
12. USDA, ERS, *World Grain Database*.
13. USDA, ERS, *Agricultural Resources: Cropland, Water, and Conservation Situation and Outlook Report*, Washington, D.C., September 1991.
14. Elizabeth Checchio, *Water Farming: The Promise and Problems of Water Transfers in Arizona* (Tucson: University of Arizona, 1988).
15. Zhores Medvedev, *The Legacy of Chernobyl* (New York: W.W. Norton & Co., 1990).

## IRRIGATION EXPANSION SLOWING

1. U.N. Food and Agriculture Organization (FAO), *Production Yearbook 1990* (Rome: 1991); Bill Quimby, Economic Research Service (ERS), U.S. Department of Agriculture (USDA), Washington, D.C., private communication, March 20, 1992.
2. FAO, *Production Yearbook 1990*; Quimby, private communication.
3. Frederick W. Crook, *Agricultural Statistics of the People's Republic of China, 1949-86* (Washington, D.C.: USDA, ERS, 1988).
4. Center for Monitoring the Indian Economy, Economic Intelligence Service, *Basic Statistics Relating to the Indian Economy, Vol. 1: All India* (Bombay: 1984).
5. FAO, *Production Yearbook* (Rome: various years).

6. Gordon Sloggett and Clifford Dickason, *Ground-Water Mining in the United States* (Washington, D.C.: USDA, ERS, 1986).
7. USDA, ERS, *USSR: Agriculture and Trade Report*, Washington, D.C., May 1988.
8. Sloggett and Dickason, *Ground-Water Mining*.
9. USDA, ERS, *China Situation and Outlook Report*, Washington, D.C., July 1987.
10. Salamat Ali, "Adrift in Flood and Drought," *Far Eastern Economic Review*, August 27, 1987.
11. Philip P. Micklin, "Desiccation of the Aral Sea: A Water Management Disaster in the Soviet Union," *Science*, September 1, 1988; Martin Walker, "Sea Turning Into Desert," *Manchester Guardian Weekly*, April 24, 1988.
12. Sandra Postel, *Water for Agriculture: Facing the Limits*, Worldwatch Paper 93 (Washington, D.C.: Worldwatch Institute, December 1989).
13. Ibid.
14. For a more detailed discussion of the changing world water situation, see Sandra Postel, *Last Oasis: Facing Water Scarcity* (New York: W.W. Norton & Co., in press).

## FERTILIZER USE FALLS

1. U.N. Food and Agriculture Organization (FAO), *Fertilizer Yearbook* (Rome: various years); The Fertilizer Institute, *Fertilizer Facts and Figures, 1990* (Washington, D.C.: 1990); U.S. Department of Agriculture (USDA), Economic Research Service (ERS), *World Grain Database* (unpublished printouts) (Washington, D.C.: 1991).
2. FAO, *Fertilizer Yearbook*; Fertilizer Institute, *Fertilizer Facts and Figures*; USDA, ERS, *World Grain Database*.
3. Lester R. Brown, "Reexamining the World Food Prospect," in Lester R. Brown et al., *State of the World 1989* (New York: W.W. Norton & Co., 1989).
4. FAO, *Fertilizer Yearbook*; Fertilizer Institute, *Fertilizer Facts and Figures*; USDA, ERS, *World Grain Database*.
5. USDA, ERS, *World Grain Database*.
6. Brown, "Reexamining the World Food Prospect."
7. FAO, *Production Yearbook 1990* (Rome: 1990).
8. Elliot Berg, "Fertilizer Subsidies" (draft), World Bank, Washington, D.C., December, 1985.
9. K.F. Isherwood and K.G. Soh, "The Medium Term Supply and Demand Prospects for Fertilizer Materials," International Fertilizer Industry Association, Paris, June 1991.
10. FAO, *Production Yearbook 1990*; Bill Quimby, USDA, ERS, Washington, D.C., private communication, March 20, 1992.

# Notes

11. Lester R. Brown, with Erik P. Eckholm, *By Bread Alone* (New York: Praeger Publishers, 1974).
12. From 1950 to 1980, U.S. fertilizer use climbed dramatically as yields responded to the application of additional fertilizer, but the failure of fertilizer use to increase at all during the eighties, even where commodity prices are favorable, indicates that yields are no longer very responsive to additional fertilizer.
13. Duane Chapman and Randy Barker, *Resource Depletion, Agricultural Research, and Development* (Ithaca, N.Y.: Cornell University, 1987).
14. Brown, "Reexamining the World Food Prospect."
15. Fertilizer usage rates in these countries are low by international standards. Agronomically all have the potential to use far more fertilizer. In Argentina, for example, simply removing the export tax on farm commodities would raise prices and boost fertilizer use.

## OIL PRODUCTION FALLS

1. American Petroleum Institute (API), *Basic Petroleum Data Book* (Washington, D.C.: 1992); British Petroleum (BP), *BP Statistical Review of World Energy* (London: 1992).
2. API, *Basic Petroleum Data Book*.
3. U.S. Department of Energy (DOE), Energy Information Administration (EIA), *Monthly Energy Review March 1992* (Washington, D.C.: 1992).
4. DOE, EIA, *Weekly Petroleum Status Report*, various issues.
5. DOE, EIA, *Monthly Energy Review March 1992*.
6. Ibid.
7. "IPAA: U.S. Oil Flow Headed for Further Decline," *Oil & Gas Journal*, May 13, 1991.
8. BP, *BP Statistical Review*.
9. Ray Moseley, "Soviet Oil Industry Suffers Deepest Crisis in its History," *Journal of Commerce*, September 17, 1991.
10. William Dawkins, "Middle East to Increase Share of Oil Output," *Financial Times*, June 4, 1991.

## NATURAL GAS PRODUCTION CLIMBS

1. American Petroleum Institute, *Basic Petroleum Data Book* (Washington, D.C.: 1992); British Petroleum, *BP Statistical Review of World Energy* (London: 1992).
2. Gregg Marland, "Carbon Dioxide Emission Rates for Conventional and Synthetic Fuels," *Energy*, Vol. 8, No. 12, 1983; natural gas often contains sulfur at the wellhead, but the sulfur is stripped out before it reaches distribution pipelines in order to avoid corrosion.
3. U.S. Department of Energy, Energy Information Administration, *Monthly Energy Review March 1992* (Washington, D.C.: 1992). The United States is one of the few countries that allows gas prices to be set by a relatively free market; others rely on state monopolies and government controls.
4. W.L. Fisher, "Factors in Realizing Future Supply Potential of Domestic Oil and Natural Gas," presented at the Aspen Institute Energy Policy Forum, Aspen, Colo., July 13, 1991.
5. Robert A. Hefner, "Natural Gas Resource Base and Production Capability Policy Issues," presented at the Aspen Institute Energy Policy Forum, Aspen, Colo., July 13, 1991.
6. "U.K. Fuel Production Up in 1991," *European Energy Report*, February 21, 1992; "U.K. Pressures Power Firms on Coal," *European Energy Report*, June 12, 1992; "U.K. Power Firms in Gas Schemes," *European Energy Report*, June 26, 1992.
7. C.D. Masters et al., "Resource Constraints in Petroleum Production Potential," *Science*, July 12, 1991.
8. Edwin Moore and Enrique Crousillat, "Prospects for Gas-Fueled Combined-Cycle Power Generation in the Developing Countries," Energy Series Paper No. 35, World Bank, Washington, D.C., 1991.
9. Russia is the largest gas producer in the Commonwealth of Independent States (the former Soviet Union), but since independent statistics for Russia are not yet available, C.I.S. totals are the best approximation.
10. "World Status: A Grid for East Asia," *Energy Economist*, February 1992.

## NUCLEAR POWER AT STANDSTILL

1. Greenpeace International, WISE-Paris, and Worldwatch Institute, *The World Nuclear Industry Status Report: 1992* (London: 1992).
2. Ibid.
3. International Atomic Energy Agency, *Annual Report* (Vienna: 1974).
4. "World List of Nuclear Power Plants," *Nuclear News*, February 1992.
5. Ibid.
6. Ibid.
7. Vladimir Chernousenko, *Chernobyl: Insight from the Inside* (New York: Springer Verlag, 1991).
8. "World List of Nuclear Power Plants," *Nuclear News*, February 1992.
9. Frederic/Schneiders, Inc., for the Safe Energy Communication Council, "Americans Speak Out on Energy Policy," Washington, D.C., March 1992; Christopher Flavin, *Nuclear Power: The Fallout from*

*Chernobyl*, Worldwatch Paper 75 (Washington, D.C.: Worldwatch Institute, March 1987).

## WIND POWER SOARS

1. American Wind Energy Association (AWEA), *1992 Wind Technology Status Report* (Washington, D.C.: 1992); Paul Gipe, AWEA, Tehachapi, Calif., private communication, April 10, 1992.
2. AWEA, *1992 Wind Technology Status Report*; Gipe, private communication.
3. AWEA, *1992 Wind Technology Status Report*.
4. U.S. Department of Energy, Energy Information Administration, *Historical Plant Cost and Annual Production Expenses for Selected Electric Plants, 1987* (Washington, D.C.: 1989).
5. Nicholas Lenssen, "California's Wind Industry Takes Off," *World Watch*, July/August 1990.
6. AWEA, *1992 Wind Technology Status Report*.
7. Ibid.
8. AWEA, *European Wind Energy Incentives* (Washington, D.C.: 1992).
9. "Europe To Out-Install U.S. in New Wind Energy Capacity," *The Solar Letter*, March 6, 1992.
10. David Stipp, " 'Wind Farms' May Energize the Midwest," *Wall Street Journal*, September 6, 1991.
11. D.L. Elliott et al., *An Assessment of the Available Windy Land Area and Wind Energy Potential in the Contiguous United States* (Richland, Wash.: Pacific Northwest Laboratory, 1991.)
12. Ibid.
13. Worldwatch Institute estimate based on Paul Gipe, "Wind Energy Comes of Age," AWEA, Tehachapi, Calif., May 13, 1991.
14. Lockheed California Company, "Wind Energy Mission Analysis," Burbank, Calif., October 1976; Matania Ginosar, "A Proposed Large-Scale Wind Energy Program for California," *Energy Sources*, Vol. 5, No. 2, 1980; Michael Dubey and Ugo Coty, *Impact of Large Wind Energy Systems in California* (Sacramento, Calif.: California Energy Commission, 1981).

## SOLAR CELL PRODUCTION EXPANDING

1. Paul Maycock, *PV News*, February 1992, February 1985, and February 1982.
2. Ken Zweibel, *Harnessing Solar Power: The Photovoltaic Challenge* (New York: Plenum Publishing, 1990).
3. Ibid.
4. Maycock, *PV News*.
5. Carl J. Weinberg and Robert H. Williams, "Energy from the Sun," *Scientific American*, September 1990.

6. "PV Shipments Up More Modestly Than Had Been Anticipated," *The Solar Letter*, February 7, 1992.
7. Ibid.
8. A.E. Cullison, "Japanese Solar Cell Producers Expand to Meet Demand Abroad," *Journal of Commerce*, March 18, 1992.
9. "Siemens, Atlantic Richfield Complete Sale of ARCO Solar; U.S. Presence Kept," *Solar Energy Intelligence Report*, February 9, 1990.
10. Neville Williams, "Solar Serendipity: Photovoltaic Rural Electrification in Sri Lanka," *Solar Today*, November/December 1991.
11. Ibid.
12. Ibid.
13. Ibid.

## ENERGY EFFICIENCY FALLS

1. British Petroleum (BP), *BP Statistical Review of World Energy* (London: various years); United Nations, Department of Economic and Social Affairs, *World Energy Supplies: 1950-1974* (New York: 1976); World Bank, Department of Socio-Economic Data, Washington, D.C., unpublished printout, February 1992; gross world product data for 1950 and 1955 from Herbert R. Block, *The Planetary Product in 1980: A Creative Pause?* (Washington, D.C.: U.S. Department of State, 1981).
2. BP, *BP Statistical Review*; World Bank, unpublished printout.
3. U.S. Department of Energy (DOE), *Monthly Energy Review March 1992* (Washington, D.C.: 1992).
4. Ashok Gadgil et al., "Advanced Lighting and Window Technologies for Reducing Electricity Consumption and Peak Demand: Overseas Manufacturing and Marketing Opportunities," Lawrence Berkeley Laboratory, Berkeley, Calif., March 1991.
5. Howard Geller, "Energy-Efficient Residential Appliances: Performance Issues and Policy Options," *IEEE Technology and Society Magazine*, March 1986.
6. Figure derived from DOE, *Monthly Energy Review March 1992*.
7. International Energy Agency (IEA), *Energy Policies of IEA Countries* (Paris: Organisation for Economic Cooperation and Development, 1991); BP, *BP Statistical Review*; International Monetary Fund (IMF), *International Financial Statistics*, June 1992.
8. IEA, *Energy Policies of IEA Countries*; BP, *BP Statistical Review*; IMF, *International Financial Statistics*.
9. BP, *BP Statistical Review of World Energy* (London: 1992).
10. Michael Philips, *The Least Cost Energy Path For Developing Countries* (Washington, D.C.: International Institute for Energy Conservation, 1991).

# Notes

11. IEA, *Energy Policies of IEA Countries*; BP, *BP Statistical Review*; IMF, *International Financial Statistics*.
12. "Environment Tax Panel Set Up," *The Daily Yomiuri*, April 16, 1992; "Commission Asked to Make Formal Proposal on Energy Tax to Address Climate Change," *International Environment Reporter*, December 18, 1991.

## GLOBAL TEMPERATURE RISES

1. Helene Wilson, NASA Goddard Institute for Space Studies, New York, private communication, March 23, 1992.
2. Ibid.; J. Hansen and S. Lebedeff, "Global Surface Air Temperatures: Update through 1987," *Geophysical Research Letters*, Vol. 15, No. 4, 1988.
3. Wilson, private communication; Hansen and Lebedeff, "Global Surface Air Temperatures."
4. Intergovernmental Panel on Climate Change (IPCC), *1992 IPCC Supplement: Working Group I Scientific Assessment of Climate Change* (Geneva and Nairobi: World Meteorological Organization and United Nations Environment Programme, 1992).
5. Department of Commerce, National Oceanic and Atmospheric Administration, National Weather Service-National Meteorological Center, Climate Analysis Center, *Weekly Climate Bulletin*, March 14, 1992.
6. Gregg Marland et al., *Estimates of $CO_2$ Emissions from Fossil Fuel Burning and Cement Manufacturing, Based on the United Nations Energy Statistics and the U.S. Bureau of Mines Cement Manufacturing Data* (Oak Ridge, Tenn.: Oak Ridge National Laboratory, 1989); R.A. Houghton et al., "The Flux of Carbon from Terrestrial Ecosystems to the Atmosphere in 1980 Due to Changes in Land Use: Geographic Distribution of the Global Flux," *Tellus*, February-April 1987.
7. Charles D. Keeling and Timothy P. Whorf, "Atmospheric $CO_2$—Modern Record, Mauna Loa," in Thomas A. Boden et al., *Trends '91: A Compendium of Data on Global Change* (Oak Ridge, Tenn.: Oak Ridge National Laboratory, 1991); Timothy P. Whorf, Scripps Institution of Oceanography, La Jolla, Calif., private communication, April 2, 1992.
8. V. Ramanathan et al., "Trace Gas Trends and Their Potential Role in Climate Change," *Journal of Geophysical Research*, June 20, 1985.
9. R. Monastersky, "Industrial Countries Warmed Most at Night," *Science News*, January 4, 1992; "Most Northern Hemisphere Warming Has Occurred at Night," *Global Environmental Change Report*, January 17, 1992.
10. IPCC, *1992 IPCC Supplement*.

## CARBON EMISSIONS STEADY

1. Carbon emissions figures are based on Gregg Marland et al., *Estimates of $CO_2$ Emissions from Fossil Fuel Burning and Cement Manufacturing, Based on the United Nations Energy Statistics and the U.S. Bureau of Mines Cement Manufacturing Data* (Oak Ridge, Tenn.: Oak Ridge National Laboratory, 1989), and on Thomas A. Boden et al., *Trends '91* (Oak Ridge, Tenn.: Oak Ridge National Laboratory, 1991). The 1990 and 1991 figures are based on British Petroleum (BP), *BP Statistical Review of World Energy* (London: 1992).
2. Marland et al., *Estimates of $CO_2$ Emissions*; R.A. Houghton et al., "The Flux of Carbon from Terrestrial Ecosystems to the Atmosphere in 1980 Due to Changes in Land Use: Geographic Distribution of the Global Flux," *Tellus*, February-April 1987.
3. "Final Conference Statement: Scientific/Technical Sessions," Second World Climate Conference, Geneva, November 7, 1990.
4. Marland et al., *Estimates of $CO_2$ Emissions*.
5. Ibid.
6. Ibid.; Boden et al., *Trends '91*; BP, *BP Statistical Review*.
7. Robert H. Williams and Eric D. Larson, "Expanding Roles for Gas Turbines in Power Generation," in Thomas B. Johansson et al., eds., *Electricity: Efficient End-Use and New Generation Technologies, and Their Planning Implications* (Lund, Sweden: Lund University Press, 1990).
8. Marland et al., *Estimates of $CO_2$ Emissions*.
9. Ibid.
10. Karen Schmidt, "Industrial Countries' Responses to Global Climate Change," *Environmental and Energy Study Institute Special Report*, Washington, D.C., July 1, 1991.

## CFC PRODUCTION FALLING FAST

1. E.I. Du Pont de Nemours, Wilmington, Del., private communication, April 15, 1992.
2. Donella Meadows et al., *Beyond the Limits* (Post Mills, Vt.: Chelsea Green Publishing Company, 1992).
3. "Scientific Assessment of Ozone Depletion: 1991," Report No. 25, World Meteorological Organization, Geneva, 1992.
4. Eloise Salholz and Mary Hager, "More Bad News in the Air," *Newsweek*, February 17, 1992.
5. "EC, Japan to Bring Forward CFC Phaseout," *Global Environmental Change Report*, February 28, 1992.

6. Mark Trumbull, "Companies Can Meet Quicker Deadline for Protecting Ozone," *Christian Science Monitor*, February 13, 1992.
7. Ibid.
8. Friends of the Earth, "Cold Comfort for the Ozone Layer: Local Authority Recovery and Recycling of CFC's From Domestic Refrigeration Equipment," London, October 1991.
9. Cynthia Pollock Shea, "Disarming Refrigerators," *World Watch*, May/June 1991.
10. James G. Anderson, "How to Find an Ozone Hole," *Wall Street Journal*, March 23, 1992.
11. Meadows et al., *Beyond the Limits*.
12. Ibid.
13. U.N. Environment Programme, "Environmental Effects of Ozone Depletion: 1991 Update," Nairobi, November 1991.
14. Meadows et al., *Beyond the Limits*.
15. Alan H. Teramura and N. S. Murali, "Intraspecific Differences in Growth and Yield of Soybean Exposed to Ultraviolet -B Radiation Under Greenhouse and Field Conditions," *Environmental and Experimental Botany*, Vol. 26, No. 1, 1986.
16. Meadows et al., *Beyond the Limits*.

## ECONOMY CONTRACTS SLIGHTLY

1. World Bank, Department of Socio-Economic Data, private communication, February 1992; International Monetary Fund (IMF), *World Economic Outlook October 1992* (Washington, D.C.: 1992).
2. Ibid.
3. Ibid.
4. Ibid.
5. Ibid.
6. World Bank, Department of Socio-Economic Data, Washington, D.C., unpublished printout, February 1992.
7. Ibid.; population data from Bureau of the Census, as as cited in Francis Urban and Philip Rose, *World Population by Country and Region, 1950-86, and Projections to 2050* (Washington, D.C.: Economic Research Service, U.S. Department of Agriculture, 1988).
8. World Bank, *World Tables 1991* (Washington, D.C.: 1991); World Bank, *World Development Report 1992* (New York: Oxford University Press, 1992).
9. World Bank, *World Tables 1991*; World Bank, *World Development Report 1992*.
10. World Bank, private communication; IMF, *World Economic Outlook October 1992*.
11. World Bank, *World Development Report 1991* (New York: Oxford University Press, 1991); Population

Reference Bureau, *1991 World Population Data Sheet* (Washington, D.C.: 1991).

## THIRD WORLD DEBT PERSISTS

1. World Bank, *World Debt Tables 1991-92, External Debt of Developing Countries* (Washington, D.C.: 1991).
2. Ibid.
3. Ibid.
4. Lester R. Brown et al., *Saving the Planet* (New York: W.W. Norton & Co., 1991).
5. World Bank, *World Debt Tables 1991-92*.
6. Ibid.; World Bank, *World Debt Tables 1989-90, External Debt of Developing Countries* (Washington, D.C.: 1989).
7. Linda Starke, *Signs of Hope* (New York: Oxford University Press, 1990).
8. Stephen Fidler, "UK Takes Unilateral Action on Debt Plan," *Financial Times*, October 18, 1991.
9. Brown et al., *Saving the Planet*.

## AUTOMOBILE PRODUCTION DROPS

1. Production in 1950-90 from Motor Vehicle Manufacturers Association (MVMA), *Facts & Figures '91* and *World Motor Vehicle Data*, 1991 edition (Detroit, Mich.: 1991); 1991 production in Japan from Japan Automobile Manufacturers Association, private communication, March 24, 1992, in United States from MVMA, private communication, March 24, 1992, in Germany from Verband der Automobilindustrie, Frankfurt, Germany, private communication, March 24, 1992, in Europe from Motor Vehicle Manufacturers Association of Italy (ANFIA), "Le Potenze Mondiali dell'Auto," Torino, Italy, 1992, in Canada from Statistics Canada, Ottawa, Canada, private communication, March 24, 1992, in Brazil, China, and South Korea from *Automotive News*, February 3, 1992, in Mexico from *Ward's Automotive Reports*, January 30, 1991, in Spain from Jose-Ramon Ferrandis, Counselor for Economic and Commercial Affairs, Embassy of Spain, Washington, D.C., private communication, March 24, 1992, and in Italy and world from ANFIA, "Le Potenze Mondiali dell'Auto" and from Worldwatch Institute estimates.
2. MVMA, private communication; ANFIA, "Le Potenze Mondiali dell'Auto"; Japan Automobile Manufacturers Association, private communication.
3. *Automotive News*, February 3, 1992.
4. Mexico from *Ward's Automotive Reports*, January 30,

1991; Spain from Ferrandis, private communication; Brazil from *Automotive News*, February 3, 1992.

5. *Automotive News*, February 3, 1992.

6. *Ward's Automotive Reports*, February 3, 1992, and *Automotive News*, January 13, 1992.

7. *Automotive News*, February 3, 1992.

8. MVMA, *Facts & Figures '91*.

9. Ibid.

10. Worldwatch Institute estimate.

11. Auto ownership is Worldwatch Institute estimate based on number of cars on the road from MVMA, *Facts & Figures '91*, from U.S. Federal Highway Administration registrations and world data in MVMA, *World Motor Vehicle Data*, and from R.L. Polk & Co., Detroit, Mich., private communication, March 24, 1992 (by permission; not for quotation without further permission), and on population estimates from Population Reference Bureau, *World Population Data Sheets* (Washington, D.C.: various years), from Population Reference Bureau, "World Population Estimates and Projections by Single Years: 1750-2100," Washington, D.C., unpublished printout, March 1992, and from U.S. Department of Commerce, Bureau of the Census, *Statistical Abstract of the United States: 1986* (Washington, D.C.: U.S. Government Printing Office, 1985).

## BICYCLE PRODUCTION OUTPACES AUTOS

1. 1990 world production figure is a Worldwatch Institute estimate based on the 1985-89 production trends of the world's top six bicycle producers; world passenger car production in 1990 was 35.7 million, according to Motor Vehicle Manufacturers Association (MVMA), *Facts and Figures '91* (Detroit, Mich.: 1991).

2. World bicycle production in 1960 was 20 million, according to United Nations, *The Growth of World Industry 1969 Edition*, Vol. II (New York: Department of Economic and Social Affairs, 1971).

3. Total of bicycles on road is a Worldwatch Institute estimate based on United Nations, *Bicycles and Components: A Pilot Survey of Opportunities for Trade Among Developing Countries* (Geneva: International Trade Center, UNCTAD/GATT, 1985), and on production data for 1985-89 from United Nations, *Industrial Statistics Yearbook 1989 Edition*, Vol. II (New York: Department of Economic and Social Affairs, 1991); number of cars on the road in 1989 was 424 million, according to MVMA, *Facts and Figures '91*; United Nations, *Industrial Statistics Yearbook 1989 Edition*.

4. Data for 1960-69 from United Nations, *Industrial Sta-*

*tistics Yearbook 1969 Edition* (New York: Department of Economic and Social Affairs, 1971); data for China from United Nations, *Industrial Statistics Yearbook 1979 Edition* (New York: Department of Economic and Social Affairs, 1981) and from United Nations, *Industrial Statistics Yearbook 1989 Edition*.

5. "Ways to Turn the Wheels of the Bicycle Industry," *China Daily*, March 14, 1990.

6. 1990 production figures from *Interbike Directory 1992* (Costa Mesa, Calif.: Primedia, Inc., 1992).

7. United Nations, *Industrial Statistics Yearbook 1989*.

8. *Interbike Directory 1992*.

9. Ibid.

10. Ibid.

11. Jiang Xiao Yun, "Nearly 2 Million Bicycles Exported," *China Daily*, December 23, 1989.

12. Sukhpal Singh, "Bicycle Industry Since Independence: Growth, Structure and Demand," *Economic and Political Weekly*, August 25, 1990.

13. *Interbike Directory 1992*.

14. Ibid.

15. MVMA, *Facts and Figures '91*; bicycle production during the sixties from United Nations, *The Growth of World Industry 1969 Edition*.

## POPULATION GROWTH SETS RECORD

1. Bureau of the Census data, as cited in Francis Urban and Philip Rose, *World Population by Country and Region, 1950-86, and Projections to 2050* (Washington, D.C.: Economic Research Service (ERS), U.S. Department of Agriculture (USDA), 1988).

2. Population Reference Bureau (PRB), *1991 World Population Data Sheet* (Washington, D.C.: 1991).

3. Ibid.

4. Ibid.; USDA, ERS, *World Grain Database* (unpublished printouts) (Washington, D.C.: 1991).

5. PRB, *1991 World Population Data Sheet*.

6. PRB, "World Population Estimates and Projections by Single Years: 1750-2100," Washington, D.C., unpublished printout, March 1992.

7. World Bank, *World Development Report 1991* (New York: Oxford University Press, 1991); PRB, *1991 World Population Data Sheet*.

8. George Tseo, "The Greening of China," *Earthwatch*, May/June 1992.

9. Jodi L. Jacobson, "Abortion in a New Light," *World Watch*, March/April 1990.

10. Jodi L. Jacobson, *The Global Politics of Abortion*, Worldwatch Paper 97 (Washington, D.C.: Worldwatch Institute, July 1990).

11. U.N. Population Fund, *State of the World's Population 1992* (New York: 1992).

## INFANT MORTALITY DECLINING

1. United Nations, *World Population Prospects 1990* (New York: 1991).
2. UNICEF, *State of the World's Children 1992* (New York: Oxford University Press, 1992).
3. Ibid.
4. World Bank, *World Development Report 1991* (New York: Oxford University Press, 1991).
5. Bob Hall and Mary Lee Kerr, *1991-92 Green Index* (Washington, D.C.: Island Press, 1991).
6. U.S. Department of Commerce, Bureau of the Census, *Statistical Abstract of the United States: 1991* (Washington, D.C.: 1991).
7. Ibid.
8. Jodi L. Jacobson, *Women's Reproductive Health: The Silent Emergency*, Worldwatch Paper 102 (Washington, D.C.: Worldwatch Institute, June 1991).
9. World Bank, *World Development Report 1991*.

## CIGARETTE SMOKING LOSING FAVOR

1. U.S. Department of Agriculture (USDA), *Tobacco Database* (unpublished printouts)(Washington, D.C.: 1991).
2. Ibid.
3. USDA, Foreign Agricultural Service, *World Tobacco Situation*, Washington, D.C., January 1992 and earlier issues.
4. USDA, *Tobacco Database*.
5. U.S. Department of Health and Human Services, *Reducing the Health Consequences of Smoking: 25 Years of Progress, A Report of the Surgeon General* (Washington, D.C.: 1989).
6. Lawrence K. Altman, "The Evidence Mounts on Passive Smoking," *New York Times*, May 29, 1990.
7. R.T. Ravenholt, "Addiction Mortality in the United States, 1980: Tobacco, Alcohol, and Other Substances," *Population and Development Review*, December 1984.
8. Peter Weber, "Last Gasp for U.S. Smokers," *World Watch*, November/December 1990.
9. Ibid.
10. Ibid.
11. David Sweanor, Canadian Non-Smoker's Rights Association, Ottawa, Ont., private communication, November 11, 1991.
12. Lori Heise, "Unhealthy Alliance," *World Watch*, September/October 1988.
13. William U. Chandler, "Banishing Tobacco," in Lester R. Brown et al., *State of the World 1986* (New York: W.W. Norton & Co., 1986).
14. Ibid.
15. Barbara Basler, "Hong Kong Reels From Rise in Cigarette Tax," *New York Times*, March 24, 1991.
16. "Japan's Cigarette Sales Reach Record Levels," *Journal of Commerce*, April 23, 1992.
17. "China Takes Aim at Tobacco," *Wall Street Journal*, October 11, 1991.

## MILITARY EXPENDITURES FALLING

1. Worldwatch Institute estimates, based on Stockholm International Peace Research Institute (SIPRI), *SIPRI Yearbook 1991: World Armaments and Disarmament* (Oxford: Oxford University Press, 1991).
2. Nicole Ball, *Security and Economy in the Third World* (Princeton, N.J.: Princeton University Press, 1988).
3. "Soviet Military Budget: $128 Billion Bombshell," *New York Times*, May 31, 1989.
4. Saadet Deger, "World Military Expenditure," in SIPRI, *SIPRI Yearbook 1991*; the annual report by the U.S. Arms Control and Disarmament Agency, *World Military Expenditures and Arms Transfers*, a widely used resource, incorporates CIA estimates of Soviet spending; for critique of CIA numbers, see Franklyn D. Holzman, "Politics and Guesswork. CIA and DIA Estimates of Soviet Military Spending," *International Security*, Fall 1989.
5. 1989 SIPRI data from Deger, "World Military Expenditure"; 1990 data from Dr. Somnath Sen, Senior Researcher, SIPRI, Stockholm, Sweden, private communication, April 7, 1992.
6. Because SIPRI does not provide figures for China, U.S. government estimates are used here to arrive at global estimates.
7. Celestine Bohlen, "New Russian Budget Is Strong Medicine," *New York Times*, January 25, 1992.
8. "National defense outlays" encompasses Department of Defense and military-related Department of Energy spending.
9. George Graham, "Cheney Concedes Ground on Costly and Controversial Programmes," *Financial Times*, January 30, 1992.
10. Helen Dewar, "Bush, Mitchell Take Aim at Slashing the Defense Budget," *Washington Post*, January 17, 1992; Patrick E. Tyler, "Top Congressman Seeks Deeper Cuts in Military Budget," *New York Times*, February 23, 1992; Dan Balz, "Harkin Urges 50% Cut in Defense Spending," *Washington Post*, January 24, 1992; "Various Congressional Budget Proposals to Cut Defense Spending," Defense Budget Project,

## Notes

Washington, D.C., January 24, 1992; Patrick E. Tyler, "U.S. Could Cut Defense Spending By More Than 33%, Report Says," *New York Times*, September 24, 1991.

11. Deger, "World Military Expenditure"; Institute for Defense and Disarmament Studies, *The Arms Control Reporter 1991*, Section 240.B (Brookline, Mass.: 1991).

12. K.K. Sharma, "Indian Budget May Cut Defence Spending," *Financial Times*, July 22, 1991.

13. Calculations are based on spending expressed in constant U.S. dollars; thus exchange-rate fluctuations may be a factor.

14. Michael G. Renner, "Swords Into Consumer Goods," *World Watch*, July/August 1989.

15. Daniel Southerland, "China Increases Spending on Military by 15 Percent," *Washington Post*, March 22, 1990; Nicholas D. Kristof, "China to Reward Army With 13% Increase in Military Budget," *New York Times*, March 22, 1992.

## NUCLEAR ARSENAL SHRINKING

1. Robert S. Norris et al., "Nuclear Weapons," in Stockholm International Peace Research Institute (SIPRI), *SIPRI Yearbook 1991: World Armaments and Disarmament* (Oxford: Oxford University Press, 1991).

2. Ibid.

3. For an overview of health and safety problems, see Michael Renner, "Assessing the Military's War on the Environment," in Lester R. Brown et al., *State of the World 1991* (New York: W.W. Norton and Co., 1991).

4. Robert S. Norris, Natural Resources Defence Council, Washington, D.C., private communication, April 1, 1992.

5. Eric Schmitt, "Cheney Orders Bombers Off Alert, Starting Sharp Nuclear Pullback," *New York Times*, September 29, 1991. Numerical reductions calculated from Norris et al., "Nuclear Weapons."

6. Eric Schmitt, "NATO to Cut Its Nuclear Bombs by Half," *New York Times*, October 12, 1991.

7. Serge Schmemann, "Gorbachev Matches U.S. on Nuclear Cuts and Goes Further on Strategic Warheads," *New York Times*, October 6, 1991.

8. Robert S. Norris and William Arkin, "Proposed U.S. and C.I.S. Strategic Forces," *Bulletin of the Atomic Scientists*, May 1992; Michael Wines, "Bush and Yeltsin Agree to Cut Long-Range Atomic Warheads; Scrap Key Land-Based Missiles," *New York Times*, June 17, 1992.

9. Jonathan Eyal and David Fairhall, "Britain Struggles

to Defend Size of Arsenal," (Manchester) *Guardian*, February 1, 1992; David White, "Britain Seeks Watertight Nuclear Deterrent," *Financial Times*, February 10, 1992; Alan Riding, "France Drops Plans to Build New Nuclear Missile System," *New York Times*, July 23, 1991.

10. Thomas B. Cochran et al., *Nuclear Weapons Databook, Vol. II: U.S. Nuclear Warhead Production* (Cambridge, Mass.: Ballinger Publishing Company, 1987).

11. Felicity Barringer, "Production of a U.S. H-Bomb to End, Official Says," *New York Times*, January 26, 1992.

12. Norris, private communication, March 17, 1992.

13. Cochran et al., *U.S. Nuclear Warhead Production*; Norris, private communication, April 1, 1992.

14. Ragnhild Ferm, "Nuclear Explosions," in SIPRI, *SIPRI Yearbook 1991*; Robert S. Norris, "Known Nuclear Tests Worldwide, 1945 to December 31, 1991," *Bulletin of the Atomic Scientists*, April 1992.

15. Alan Riding, "France Suspends Its Testing of Nuclear Weapons," *New York Times*, April 9, 1992.

## BIRDS FAST DISAPPEARING

1. Nigel Collar, International Council for Bird Preservation, Cambridge, U.K., private communication, March 31, 1992.

2. Ibid.

3. Jared M. Diamond, "Twilight of Hawaiian Birds," *Nature*, October 10, 1991.

4. Frank Graham, Jr., "2001: Birds That Won't Be With Us," *American Birds*, Winter 1990.

5. Chandler S. Robbins et al., "Population Declines in North American Birds that Migrate to the Neotropics," Proceedings of the National Academy of Sciences, Washington, D.C., June 29, 1989.

6. Rob Fuller et al., "Feeding the Birds Down on the Farm: Perspectives from Britain," *Ambio*, September 1991.

7. Figure derived from duck breeding population graphs in J. Bradley Bortner et al., "1991 Status of Waterfowl and Fall Flight Forecast," Office of Migratory Bird Management, U.S. Fish and Wildlife Service, Laurel, Md., 1991.

8. Michael Mozar, Director, International Waterfowl and Wetlands Research Bureau, Gloucester, U.K., private communication, February 13, 1990.

9. Graham, "2001: Birds That Won't Be With Us."

10. Harry M. Ohlendorf et al., "Relationships Between Selenium Concentrations and Avian Reproduction," in *Transmissions of the 51st North American Wildlife and Natural Resource Conference*, Wildlife Management Institute, Washington, D.C., 1986.

11. Donald H. White et al., "Significance of Organochlorine and Heavy Metal Residues in Wintering Shorebirds at Corpus Christi, Texas, 1976-77," *Pesticides Monitoring Journal*, September 1980.

12. "Watch the Birdie," *The Economist*, August 20, 1988.

13. Edward Flickinger et al., "Bird Poisoning from Misuse of the Carbamate Furadan in a Texas Rice Field," *Wildlife Society Bulletin*, Vol. 14, 1986.

14. Humphrey Crick, "Poisoned Prey in the Heart of Africa," *New Scientist*, November 24, 1990.

15. Ibid.

16. Edward Wolf, "Survival of the Rarest," *World Watch*, March/April 1991.

17. Colin Bibby et al., "Putting Biodiversity on the Map: Priority Areas for Global Conservation," International Council for Bird Preservation, Cambridge, U.K., May 1992.

## FORESTS SHRINKING AT RECORD RATE

1. Preagricultural number from E. Matthews, "Global Vegetation and Land Use," *Journal of Climate and Applied Meteorology*, Vol. 22, 1983; current number from R. Persson, unpublished report to the Swedish International Development Authority (1985) as cited in World Resources Institute/International Institute for Environment and Development, *World Resources 1986* (New York: Basic Books, 1986).

2. U.N. Food and Agriculture Organization, *Tropical Forest Resources*, Forestry Paper 30 (Rome: 1982).

3. "New Deforestation Rate Figures Announced," Tropical Forest Programme (IUCN Newsletter), August 1990.

4. B. Bowander, "Deforestation Around Urban Centres in India," *Environmental Conservation*, Spring 1987.

5. For a listing of studies documenting secondary damage from selective logging, see Norman Myers, *The Primary Source: Tropical Forests and Our Future* (New York: W.W. Norton & Co, 1984).

6. Norman Myers, "The Hamburger Connection: How Central America's Forests Become North America's Hamburgers," *Ambio*, Vol 10, No. 1, 1981: H. Jefferey Leonard, *Natural Resources and Economic Development in Central America* (Washington, DC: International Institute for Environment and Development, 1987); Philip M. Fearnside, "Land-Use Trends in the Brazilian Amazon Region as Factors in Accelerating Deforestation," *Environmental Conservation*, Summer 1983.

7. F.C. Hummel, "In the Forests of the EEC," *Unasylva*, No. 138, 1982.

8. International Institute for Environmental Studies, *European Environmental Yearbook 1987* (London: DocTer International UK Ltd., 1987).

9. International Co-operative Programme on Assessment and Monitoring of Air Pollution Effects on Forests, "Forest Damage and Air Pollution: Report on the 1986 Forest Damage Survey in Europe," Global Environment Monitoring System, United Nations Environment Programme, Nairobi, mimeographed, 1987.

10. Forest area declined from 385 million hectares in 1630 to 249 million hectares in 1920 according to U.S. Department of Agriculture (USDA), U.S. Forest Service, *Timber Resources for America's Future*, Forest Resources Report No. 14 (Washington, D.C.: U.S. Government Printing Office, 1958). Forest area in 1982 adapted from U.S. Forest Service, *America's Renewable Resources: A Supplement to the 1979 Assessment of Forest and Rangeland in the U.S.* (Washington, D.C.: USDA, 1984); note that figure cited in text omits forest area for Alaska and Hawaii. Total U.S. forest area of United States in 1963 was approximately 307 million hectares according to USDA, U.S. Forest Service, *Timber Trends in the U.S.*, Forest Resources Report No. 17 (Washington, D.C.: U.S. Government Printing Office, 1965); forest area of contiguous states in 1963 was estimated by subtracting the 48 million hectares of forest listed for Alaska and an additional 804,000 hectares to approximate the forest area of Hawaii.

## U.S. SOIL EROSION CUT

1. U.S. Department of Agriculture (USDA), Economic Research Service (ERS), *Agricultural Resources: Cropland, Water and Conservation Situation Outlook Report*, Washington, D.C., September 1990.

2. Author's estimate.

3. USDA, *The Soil and Water Resources Conservation Act: 1980 Appraisal, Part II* (Washington, D.C.: 1980).

4. K.G. Tegwani, Land Use Consultants International, New Delhi, private communication, July 3, 1983; Center for Science and Environment, *The State of India's Environment 1982* (New Delhi: 1982).

5. S.A. El-Swaify and E.W. Dangler, "Rainfall Erosion in the Tropics: A State of the Art," in American Society of Agronomy, *Soil Erosion and Conservation in the Tropics* (Madison, Wisc.: 1982); author's personal experience and various reports in *China Daily*.

6. P. Poletayev and S. Yashukova, "Environmental Protection and Agricultural Production," *Ekonomika Sel-skogo Khozyaystva* (Moscow), November 1978; P. S. Tregubov, "Soil Rainstorm Erosion and Its Control in the U.S.S.R.," presented to the International Con-

ference on Soil Erosion and Conservation, Honolulu, Hawaii, January 16-22, 1983.

7. Donald Worster, *Dust Bowl* (New York: Oxford University Press, 1979).

8. These and other conservation practices introduced in the thirties are discussed in Worster, *Dust Bowl*, especially in Chapter 14, "Making Two Blades of Grass Grow."

9. M.F. Miller, "Cropping Systems and Erosion Control," Missouri Experiment Station Bulletin 366 (1936), reprinted in "Soil Degradation: Affects on Agricultural Productivity," *National Agricultural Land Study* (Washington, D.C.: USDA, 1980).

10. Leon Lyles, "Possible Effects of Wind Erosion on Soil Productivity," *Journal of Soil and Water Conservation*, November/December 1975.

11. USDA, ERS, *World Grain Database* (unpublished printouts) (Washington, D.C.: 1991).

12. USDA, ERS, *Agricultural Resources: Cropland, Water, and Conservation Situation Outlook Report*.

13. Lester R. Brown, "Breakthrough on Soil Erosion," *World Watch*, May/June 1988.

14. USDA, ERS, *Agricultural Resources: Cropland, Water and Conservation Situation and Outlook Report*, Washington, D.C., September 1991.

15. USDA, ERS, *Agricultural Resources: Cropland, Water and Conservation Situation and Outlook Report*, September 1990.

16. USDA, ERS, *Agricultural Resources: Cropland, Water and Conservation Situation and Outlook Report*, September 1991.

17. USDA, ERS, *Agricultural Resources: Cropland, Water, and Conservation Situation Outlook Report*, September 1990.

18. USDA, ERS, *World Grain Database*.

STEEL RECYCLING RISING SLOWLY

1. William U. Chandler, *Energy Productivity: Key to Environmental Protection and Economic Progress*, Worldwatch Paper 63 (Washington, D.C.: Worldwatch Institute, January 1985).

2. The rate for scrap is "purchased scrap," which is the steel recollected from consumers; the tons cited are short tons (2,000 pounds); U.S. Bureau of Mines, *Mineral Commodity Summaries 1991* (Washington, D.C.: 1991).

3. José Goldemberg et al., "Brazil: A Study on End-Use Energy Strategy," presented at the Global Workshop on End-Use Energy Strategies, São Paulo, Brazil, June 4-15, 1984; U.N. Economic Commission for Europe, *An Energy Efficient Future: Prospects for Europe and North America* (London: Butterworths, 1983); World Bank, *Energy Efficiency in the Steel Industry with Emphasis on the Developing Countries* (Washington, D.C.: 1984).

4. Robert Cowles Letcher and Mary T. Sheil, "Source Separation and Citizen Recycling," in William D. Robinson, ed., *The Solid Waste Handbook* (New York: John Wiley & Sons, 1986).

5. Bureau of Mines, *Mineral Commodity Summaries 1991* (Washington, D.C.: Bureau of Mines, 1991).

6. Andrea N. Ketoff, "Facts and Prospects of the Italian End-Use Energy Structure," presented at the Global Workshop on End-Use Energy Strategies, São Paulo, Brazil, June 4-15, 1984; Spain's efficiency in steel making from World Bank, *Energy Efficiency in the Steel Industry*.

7. World Bank, *Energy Efficiency in the Steel Industry*.

8. U.S. Congress, Office of Technology Assessment, *Industrial Energy Use* (Washington, D.C.: U.S. Government Pritnting Office, 1983).

9. Chandler, *Energy Productivity*.

10. Donald F. Barnett and Robert W. Crandall, *Up From The Ashes: The Rise Of The Steel Minimill In The United States* (Washington, D.C.: Brookings Institution, 1986).

11. Ibid.

12. Ibid.

13. Martin Brown and Bruce McKern, *Aluminum, Copper And Steel In Developing Countries* (Paris: OECD Development Centre, 1987).

14. Steve Apotheker, "Looking for Steel Cans," *Resource Recycling*, February 1992.

15. Marc Ross, University of Michigan, Ann Arbor, Mich., private communication, March 24, 1992.

NUCLEAR WASTE ACCUMULATING

1. Irradiated fuel figures of 9,500 and 84,000 tons are Worldwatch Institute estimates based on I.W. Leigh and S.J. Mitchell, Pacific Northwest Laboratory, *International Nuclear Fuel Cycle Fact Book* (Springfield, Va.: National Technical Information Service, 1990), on Organisation for Economic Co-operation and Development, Nuclear Energy Agency, *Nuclear Spent Fuel Management: Experience and Options* (Paris: 1986), on Andrew Blowers et al., *The International Politics of Nuclear Waste* (New York: St. Martin's Press, 1991), on Soviet figures from G.A. Kaurov, Director of the Center of Public Information for Atomic Energy, Moscow, in letter to Lydia Popova, Socio-Ecological Union, Moscow, August 5, 1991, and on East European production based on United Nations,

*Energy Statistics Yearbook* (New York: various years), on British Petroleum, *BP Statistical Review of World Energy* (London: 1991), and on above sources.

2. U.S. Department of Energy, Office of Civilian Radioactive Waste Management, *Integrated Data Base for 1990: U.S. Spent Fuel and Radioactive Waste Inventories, Projections, and Characteristics* (Washington, D.C.: 1990).

3. Frank L. Parker et al., *The Disposal of High-level Radioactive Waste 1984*, Vol. II (Stockholm: Beijer Institute, 1984); National Research Council (NRC), Board on Radioactive Waste Management (BRWM), "Rethinking High-Level Radioactive Waste Disposal," National Academy Press, Washington, D.C., July 1990.

4. Frank L. Parker et al., *The Disposal of High-level Radioactive Waste 1984*, Vol. I (Stockholm: Beijer Institute, 1984).

5. Carole Douglis, "Stones that Speak to the Future," *OMNI*, November 1985.

6. Konrad B. Krauskopf, "Disposal of High-Level Nuclear Waste: Is It Possible?" *Science*, September 14, 1990.

7. NRC, BRWM, "Rethinking High-Level Radioactive Waste Disposal."

8. Cited in Fred C. Shapiro, *Radwaste* (New York: Random House, 1981).

9. Cited in Luther J. Carter, *Nuclear Imperatives and Public Trust: Dealing with Radioactive Waste* (Washington, D.C.: Resources for the Future, 1987).

10. Diane M. Cameron and Barry D. Solomon, "Nuclear Waste Landscapes," in J. Barry Cullingworth, ed., *Energy, Land, and Public Policy* (New Brunswick, N.J.: Transaction Books, 1990).

11. Keith Schneider, "Military Has New Strategic Goal in Cleanup of Vast Toxic Waste," *New York Times*, August 5, 1991; U.S. Congress, Office of Technology Assessment, *Complex Cleanup: The Environmental Legacy of Nuclear Weapons Production* (Washington, D.C.: U.S. Government Printing Office, 1991).

12. Ann MacLachlan, "French Government Stops Test Drilling at Waste Sites for 'At Least' a Year," *Nuclear Fuel*, February 19, 1990.

13. "France Passes New Law on Disposal of Nuclear Waste Underground," *European Energy Report*, July 12, 1991.

14. Arjun Makhijani and Scott Saleska, *High-Level Dollars, Low-Level Sense: A Critique of Present Policy for the Management of Long-Lived Radioactive Wastes and Discussion of an Alternative Approach* (New York: Apex Press, 1991); Victor Gilinsky, "Nuclear Power: What Must Be Done?" *Public Utilities Fortnightly*, June 1, 1991.

15. "World Status of Radioactive Waste Management,"

*IAEA Bulletin*, Spring 1986; Leigh and Mitchell, *International Nuclear Fuel Cycle Fact Book*.

16. Bernd Franke and Arjun Makhijani, "Avoidable Death: A Review of the Selection and Characterization of a Radioactive Waste Repository in West Germany," Institute for Energy and Environmental Research, Takoma Park, Md., November 1987; Blowers et al., *The International Politics of Nuclear Waste*.

17. "HLW Disposal Plans Come to Light," *Nuke Info Tokyo*, November/December 1989.

18. "Hokkaido Government Opposes HLW Plan in Horonobe," *Nuke Info Tokyo*, September/October 1990.

19. "German Spent Fuel May Go to China," *Nuclear News*, October 1985.

20. "Joint Research Agreement Reached with China on HLW Disposal," *Nuke Info Tokyo*, November/December 1990.

21. Makhijani and Saleska, *High-Level Dollars, Low-Level Sense*; Frank L. Parker et al., *Technical and Sociopolitical Issues in Radioactive Waste Disposal*, Vol. I (Stockholm: Beijer Institute, 1987).

## ARMS TRADE EXCEEDS GRAIN

1. U.S. Arms Control and Disarmament Agency (ACDA), *World Military Expenditures and Arms Transfers 1990* (Washington, D.C.: U.S. Government Printing Office, 1991); U.S. Department of Agriculture (USDA), *World Grain Database* (unpublished printouts) (Washington, D.C.: 1990).

2. ACDA, *World Military Expenditures and Arms Transfers 1990*; conversion of 1989 dollars into 1990 dollars by the author.

3. Ibid.

4. Ian Anthony et al., "The Trade in Major Conventional Weapons," in Stockholm International Peace Research Institute (SIPRI), *SIPRI Yearbook 1991: World Armaments and Disarmament* (Oxford: Oxford University Press, 1991).

5. "Jelzin: Rußland ist auf den Waffenhandel Angewiesen," *Süddeutsche Zeitung*, February 24, 1992.

6. Worldwatch Institute calculations, based on International Monetary Fund, *International Finance Statistics, 1992* (Washington, D.C.: 1992), and on USDA, *World Grain Database*.

7. ACDA, *World Military Expenditures and Arms Transfers 1990*.

8. USDA, *World Grain Situation and Outlook*, Washington, D.C., March 1992.

9. SIPRI, *SIPRI Yearbook 1988: World Armaments and*

# Notes

*Disarmament* (Oxford: Oxford University Press, 1988).

10. Ibid.

11. SIPRI, *SIPRI Yearbook 1991*.

## WHEAT/OIL EXCHANGE RATE SHIFTS

1. U.N. Food and Agriculture Organization, *Production Yearbook 1990* (Rome: 1990).

2. British Petroleum Ltd. (BP), *BP Statistical Review of World Energy* (London: 1991).

3. U.S. Department of Agriculture (USDA), Foreign Agricultural Service (FAS), *World Rice Reference Tables* (unpublished printout) (Washington, D.C.: 1991); USDA, FAS, *World Wheat and Coarse Grains Reference Tables* (unpublished printout) (Washington, D.C.: 1991); BP, *BP Statistical Review*.

4. USDA, FAS, *World Rice Reference Tables*; USDA, FAS, *World Wheat and Coarse Grains Reference Tables*.

5. USDA, Economic Research Service, *World Grain Situation Outlook*, Washington, D.C., March 1992 and earlier editions.

## INCOME DISTRIBUTION WORSENING

1. Economy, energy, and industry from Jim MacNeill, "Strategies for Sustainable Economic Development," *Scientific American*, September 1989; distance traveled from Richard Critchfield, "Science and the Villager: The Last Sleeper Wakes," *Foreign Affairs*, Fall 1982.

2. Billionaires from Alan Farnham, "The Billionaires: Do They Pay Their Way?" *Fortune*, September 11, 1989; millionaires estimated from John Steele Gordon, "Why It Costs So Much to Be Rich," *Washington Post*, May 21, 1989; homeless from U.N. Centre for Human Settlements, New York, private communication, November 1, 1989.

3. Diet expenditures from Calorie Control Council, Atlanta, Ga., private communication, October 4, 1989; undernutrition estimated from World Bank, *Poverty and Hunger: Issues and Options for Food Security in Developing Countries* (Washington, D.C.: 1986).

4. Drinking water and sanitation based on UNICEF, *State of the World's Children 1989* (New York: Oxford University Press, 1989), and World Bank, *Social Indicators of Development 1988* (Baltimore, Md.: Johns Hopkins University Press, 1988).

5. Military expenditures estimated from U.S. Arms Control and Disarmament Agency, *World Military Expenditures and Arms Transfers 1988* (Washington,

D.C.: U.S. Government Printing Office, 1989); child mortality and cost of prevention from UNICEF, *State of the World's Children 1989*.

6. Robert S. McNamara, *The McNamara Years at the World Bank: Major Policy Addresses of Robert S. McNamara 1968-1981* (Baltimore, Md.: Johns Hopkins University Press, 1981).

7. World Bank, *World Development Report 1991* (New York: Oxford University Press, 1991).

8. World Bank, *World Tables 1991* (Washington, D.C.: 1991).

9. Robert Summers and Alan Heston, "A New Set of International Comparisons of Real Product and Price Level Estimates for 130 Countries, 1950-1985," *Review of Income and Wealth*, March 1988; Alan Heston, University of Pennsylvania, Philadelphia, Pa., private communication, September 22, 1989.

10. Income distribution figures tend to understate disparities because they are calculated for households despite differences in household size (poor households are usually larger). Share of population below average income and data in Table 1 from World Bank, *World Development Report 1988* (New York: Oxford University Press, 1988); World Resources Institute, *World Resources 1988-89* (New York: Basic Books, 1988); Agha M. Ghouser, "Urban Poverty and Unemployment in Pakistan," *Pakistan & Gulf Economist*, December 31, 1988; Joel Bergsman, *Income Distribution and Poverty in Mexico*, Staff Working Paper 395 (Washington, D.C.: World Bank, 1980); Robert D. Hamrin, "Sorry Americans—You're Still Not 'Better Off'," *Challenge*, September/October 1988; Soviet Union estimated from William U. Chandler, *Changing Role of the Market in National Economies*, Worldwatch Paper 72 (Washington, D.C.: Worldwatch Institute, September 1986).

11. World Bank, *World Development Report 1988*.

12. Ronald V.A. Sprout and James H. Weaver, "International Distribution of Income: 1960-1987," Working Paper No. 159, Department of Economics, American University, Washington, D.C., May 1991.

## MATERNAL MORTALITY TAKES HEAVY TOLL

1. World Health Organization (WHO), *Classification of Diseases: Manual of the International Statistical Classification of Diseases, Injuries, and Causes of Death*, 9th rev. (Geneva: 1987).

2. Julia A. Walsh et al., "Maternal and Perinatal Health" (draft) in D.T. Jamison and W.H. Mosley, eds., *Disease Control Priorities in Developing Countries* (Washington, D.C.: World Bank, forthcoming).

3. Ann Starrs, *Preventing the Tragedy of Maternal Deaths: A Report on the International Safe Motherhood Conference* (Nairobi: WHO, 1987).
4. WHO, *Maternal Mortality Rates: A Tabulation of Available Information* (Geneva: 1986).
5. Starrs, *Preventing the Tragedy*.
6. Distribution of number of maternal deaths by region from ibid.; share of maternal deaths in six countries of South Asia from George Acsadi and Gwendolyn Johnson-Acsadi, "Safe Motherhood in South Asia: Sociocultural and Demographic Aspects of Maternal Health," background paper prepared for the Safe Motherhood—South Asia Conference, Lahore, Pakistan, 1990.
7. Walsh et al., "Maternal and Perinatal Health."
8. Beverly Winikoff et al., "Medical Services to Save Mother's Lives: Feasible Approaches to Reducing Maternal Mortality," presented at the Safe Motherhood International Conference, Nairobi, Kenya, 1987.
9. Jodi L. Jacobson, *The Global Politics of Abortion*, Worldwatch Paper 97 (Washington, D.C.: Worldwatch Institute, July 1990).
10. Walsh et al., "Maternal and Perinatal Health."
11. Acsadi and Johnson-Acsadi, "Safe Motherhood in South Asia."
12. E. DeMaeuer and M. Adiels-Tegman, "The Prevalence of Anemia in the World," *World Health Statistics Quarterly*, Vol. 38, 1985.
13. Walsh et al., "Maternal and Perinatal Health Care."
14. Share of births assisted by trained attendants from Starrs, *Preventing the Tragedy*.
15. WHO and the International Federation of Gynaecology and Obstetrics, "Traditional Birth Attendants: A Resource for the Health of Women," *International Journal of Gynaecology and Obstetrics*, Vol. 23, 1985; A. Mangay Maglacas and John Simons, eds., *The Potential of the Traditional Birth Attendant* (Geneva: WHO, 1986).

## COERCED MOTHERHOOD INCREASING

1. Jodi L. Jacobson, *Women's Reproductive Health: The Silent Emergency*, Worldwatch Paper 102 (Washington, D.C.: Worldwatch Institute, June 1991).
2. Marsha Freeman, "Women's Human Rights and Reproductive Rights: STATUS, CAPACITY AND CHOICE," *Bulletin of the Inter-American Parliamentary Group on Population and Development*, October 1991.
3. World Health Organization, "Primary Health Care: Report on the International Conference on Primary Health Care," *Health for All*, Series No. 1, 1978.
4. Jacobson, *Women's Reproductive Health: The Silent Emergency*.
5. George Acsadi and Gwendolyn Johnson-Acsadi, "Safe Motherhood in South Asia: Sociocultural and Demographic Aspects of Maternal Health," background paper perpared for the Safe Motherhood—South Asia Conference, Lahore, Pakistan, 1990.
6. "African Customs Increase Dangers of the AIDS Epidemic," Women's International Network News (WINNEWS), Winter 1991.
7. "Machismo in Mexico," WINNEWS, Winter 1991.
8. U.N. Population Fund, *State of the World's Population 1992* (New York: 1992).
9. Elise F. Jones et al., "Fertility, Pregnancy, and Contraceptive Use," in *Pregnancy, Contraception and Family Planning Services in Industrialized Countries* (New Haven, Conn.: Yale University Press, 1989).
10. For a full report on the gang rape of Kenyan schoolgirls see *WINNEWS*, Autumn 1991.
11. Jodi L. Jacobson, *The Global Politics of Abortion*, Worldwatch Paper 97 (Washington, D.C.: Worldwatch Institute, July 1990).
12. Tomas Frejka, *Induced Abortion and Fertility: A Quarter Century of Experience in Eastern Europe*, Center for Policy Studies, Working Paper No. 99 (New York: The Population Council, 1983).
13. Worldwatch Institute estimate based on data from Stanley K. Henshaw, "Induced Abortion: A World Review, 1990," *Family Planning Perspectives*, March/April 1990; Henry David, *Abortion Research Notes*, various issues; Henry David, "Abortion in Europe, 1920-91: A Public Health Perspective," *Studies in Family Planning*, January/February 1992.
14. Frejka, *Induced Abortion and Fertility*; Henshaw, "Induced Abortion: A World Review, 1990."
15. V. Fauveau and T. Blanchet, "Deaths from Injuries and Induced Abortion Among Rural Bangladeshi Women," *Social Science in Medicine*, Vol. 29, 1989.